In the series
Women in the Political Economy,
edited by Ronnie J. Steinberg

Kevin D. Henson

Just a Temp

 Temple University Press / Philadelphia

Temple University Press, Philadelphia 19122
Copyright © 1996 by Temple University. All rights reserved
Published 1996
Printed in the United States of America

☺ The paper used in this book meets the requirements
of the American National Standard for Information Sciences—
Permanence of Paper for Printed Library Materials,
ANSI Z39.48-1984
Text design by William Boehm

Library of Congress Cataloging-in-Publication Data
Henson, Kevin Daniel, 1963–
    Just a temp / Kevin Daniel Henson.
        p.   cm. — (Women in the political economy)
    Includes bibliographical references and index.
    ISBN 1-56639-385-X (cloth: alk. paper). — ISBN 1-56639-386-8 (paper: alk.
paper)
    1. Temporary employment—United States.   2. Women—Employment—United
States.   I. Title.   II. Series.
HD5854.2.U6H46   1996
331.25'72—dc20   95-16814

For my mother, Lillian Henson,
and my father, Billy Charles Henson

Contents

Preface

So this is where the brain starts to shut down and that which we treasure most, our personal identities, begins to slip away. Here. In front of the VDT (very disturbing tormentor or video display terminal—I don't remember which), where our eyes begin to fail us and our backs become permanently hunched. I suppose I should be thankful; it's a paycheck. But this open room without windows, up on 10, behind accounting, with the Authorized Personnel Only sign on the door, is deadening to the senses. And to the spirit. A banner at the front of the room reads, "Work Smarter, Not Harder." And the only decoration, a watercolor of Sacré-Coeur on the wall (a cheap framed copy of a super-market original), serves to emphasize the bleakness.

How did I get here? I remember going from one temp agency to another in the bright afternoon sunlight (was it only yesterday?), filling out form after form and typing banal stories about getting along with others in the workplace while being timed by an invisible timer in the other room. Before I knew it, I was talking up my data entry experience (one of the more boring tasks, if they can be rated in any kind of meaningful order, from my time as an insurance clerk) and accepting an assignment in the credit department of a large national department store. "You have to be able to take this assignment for four weeks. If you can't commit to it, just say so now and we'll find you something else," my temporary counselor told me. I committed myself for $6.50 an hour. I sold myself into VDT slavery.

* * *

Thus I began my not-so-illustrious career as a temporary employee. It was the summer of 1988, the first summer of my graduate school career. I had looked in vain for an academically oriented summer job: a summer teaching post, a research position, even a job at the campus library. Finally, believing that I could "always do temp work," I began making the rounds of various Chicago Loop–based temporary agencies. There were plenty to choose from.

Indeed, Chicago was an early leader in the temporary industry. Four of the eight nationally operating temporary agencies in the early 1960s— Comptometer Corporation, Labor Pool, Statistical Tabulating Corporation, and Workman Diversified—were based in Chicago (Moore 1963). Between 1986 and 1987 temporary employment was the leading growth industry in the city, increasing an astounding 38 percent in one year (Economic Development Commission of the City of Chicago 1990, 15). In 1987 Chicago employed the third largest temporary labor force (18,045), behind only New York and Los Angeles (U.S. Department of Labor, Bureau of Labor Statistics, 1988, 27). In 1988, as I leafed through the Chicago Area Yellow Pages, I found more than 150 separate temporary agencies.

It was relatively easy to find that first temporary assignment, although the position was less than ideal in terms of wages and work satisfaction; I was "sent out" the very next day. I began keeping "field notes" on my temporary experiences immediately. Although I had sought out temporary work for survival wages, I began framing my experience, both to myself and to others, as "research." I believe now that this was a coping strategy, a kind of personal ideological work, to maintain my sense of self against the onslaught of condescension I was experiencing on the job. I ended up working for two different agencies that first summer.

The following summer, circumstances found me working for yet a third temporary agency, one recommended to me by a graduate student from the history department who had been moonlighting during the academic year to supplement the university's meager graduate student stipend. Overall, my experience with temporary work, and this agency in particular, although still problematic, was significantly more pleasant than had been my experiences the previous summer. I continued to take field notes, although I still had no intention of making temporary work the focus of my research.

For the 1990-91 academic year, however, the sociology department offered me a lectureship (three courses) for the salary of a teaching assistant. At this juncture I began seriously considering a work-and-occupations study for my dissertation, as much for financial reasons as for intellectual ones. I had been interested for some time in the social construction of personal identity and, given my previous experience in the field, temporary work seemed an ideal setting in which to undertake a closer examination. I accepted partial "funding" from my department (two evening division courses) and, telling myself that I was following a long line of Chicago School sociologists, wrote an active participant-observation component into my dissertation proposal.

In October 1990, with two summers of temporary work already completed, I reactivated my file with Right Temporaries for the year. It was through this agency that I did the majority of my participant-observation work. Ultimately, I worked a total of eighteen months as a temporary, accumulating more than 150 days of on-assignment experience in more than thirty Chicago Loop offices. I worked for both large and small organizations, from an office with only one other person to multinational corporations employing thousands of people. I worked in accounting, advertising, banking, communications, educational, financial, insurance, legal, marketing, media, medical, nonprofit, publishing, real estate, and retail organizations and institutions.

Although my research was not undercover (I did not pretend to be anyone other than myself, and I did not disguise my background), my temporary counselors were unaware that I was researching temporary work until near the end of my tenure as a temporary employee. Thus, although other factors such as my gender, race, age, education, and particular competencies may have influenced the assignments I was given, I do not believe that my research role, per se, affected the types of experiences and settings to which I was exposed. Although I occasionally did data entry and other routine assignments, I generally worked in higher-wage ($10-to-$12-an-hour) secretarial and word processing assignments.

The ratio of information gathered to time spent in "the field" (in this case usually nine to five), however, was relatively low. Interaction with supervisors, full-time employees, and other temporaries was, for the most part, limited. In addition, I was often physically isolated from others in the office and constrained in my movement around the workplace (in my role as a temporary I was frequently required to alert others whenever I left my desk). My "acceptance" in the setting, in other words, was a full day of often monotonous work.[1] Although interesting interactions and events did occur, they were ripples in a sea of otherwise often numbing sameness. My participant-observation work did, however, keep me in touch with my research interests, provide contacts, assist in the formulation of working hypotheses and interview questions, and provide a low-commitment income source.

In addition to my participant-observation work, I conducted a set of open-ended, semistructured interviews. I formally interviewed thirty-five people intimately familiar with temporary work, primarily temporary workers. I met them on assignment or contacted them through responses to fliers I placed at temporary agency offices and through referrals.[2] Of the interviewees, twenty-one were female and ten were male temporaries: All but three African-American women, one African-American man, and one Asian-American woman were white. Ages ranged from twenty to forty-five years. Collectively, my respondents worked for more than ten temporary agencies, including the three largest national agencies and a variety of medium to small local agencies. In addition, I interviewed three "temporary counselors" and one client company representative responsible for "ordering" and supervising temporary employees.

* * *

I was fortunate to have the advice, support, and encouragement of my teachers, colleagues, friends, and family during the writing of this book. Special thanks go to my mentor, Arlene Kaplan Daniels. Arlene Daniels was there to "take my temperature," hold my hand, and prod me through the various stages of the research and writing. In addition to her prompt reading of multiple drafts and many sociological insights about the world of work, I am grateful to Arlene for providing a crucial and saving sushi lunch at my lowest point in the project. Her intellectual and emotional support ensured the completion of this work. I also thank the other members of my dissertation committee, Howard Becker and Bernard Beck, for helpful comments, suggestions, and guidance during all aspects of the research, particularly during the field research and early writing periods.

Throughout the writing of this book I was lucky to have many friends and colleagues with whom to discuss my emerging thoughts about temporary work. My colleagues at Northwestern—Kelly Devers, Amy Lusk, Darrell Moore, Kirk Pillow, Diane Rothschild, Rebecca Wallin, and Sarah Willie—provided encouragement, advice, and other forms of assistance. Mitchell Stevens in particular shared his good food, wine, and conversation with me as the work evolved. Michael Reynolds, a cherished friend and a critical scholar from the "other" Chicago university, offered detailed comments, perceptive conversation, and emotional sustenance throughout the project.

New friends and colleagues in California saw me through the end stages of the project. Richard Bernard, Peggy Compton, and Allen LeBlanc read and commented on parts of the work. Mark Kowalewski provided invaluable help in the later writing stages, urging me to completion, reading drafts of each chapter, and providing voluminous editorial and theoretical suggestions.

The book in its final form benefited from the contributions of Michael Ames of Temple University Press; Ronnie Steinberg, the editor of the Women in the Political Economy series; Kim Vivier, whose thoroughness as a copy editor I greatly appreciated; Joan Vidal, the production editor; and the staff at Temple University Press.

For helping me maintain my sanity and for not asking, "Have you finished yet?" too often, I thank my friends Nick Agoff, Laura Ellen Beyer, Angelee Kovach, Vince Kracht, Andrew London, Sonja Russell, and Martin Stern.

Finally, I thank my parents, Billy C. Henson and Lillian Henson, who supported me emotionally and occasionally financially through the sometimes befuddling and seemingly never-ending process of graduate school. After a lifetime in the automobile industry of Flint, Michigan, my parents provided me with a wealth of knowledge and insights about the world of work and its organization. Although they had little experience in book production, they shared their wisdom about the completion of other large projects. I remember and cherish in particular the encouragement and support my mother provided through the metaphor of her favorite pursuit—quilting: Little by little, stitch by stitch, patch by patch, the quilt comes together until it is completed.

Finally, although their names must remain confidential, I am indebted to the women and men who graciously agreed to be interviewed for this study. I offer them my gratitude and encouragement in the search for a satisfying and fulfilling work life.

Just a Temp

1 *Introduction*

And you have all these people say, "When are you going to get a real job?" I mean, you're going through all the motions of a real job. I mean, you're showing up at a place between eight and five. And technically, you're probably doing as much as anyone else who works there full-time. You know? But you're just sort of this ghost. And you don't have a real life. And what goes along with the territory is this low-level depression. And you can't put a finger on it. An erosion of self-esteem. (Helen)

American notions of what constitutes a "real job" are based on a post–World War II model of full-time employment with implied permanency, steady and predictable wages, internal advancement and training opportunities, and the provision of employer-sponsored fringe benefits. Ideally, such real jobs are also a basis of personal identity, self-expression, and individual fulfillment. Though close to 83 percent of all working Americans were employed on a full-time basis in 1992 (U.S. Department of Commerce 1993, 402), an increasingly large segment of the U.S. work force is being hired on a temporary, part-time, contractual, or leased basis. For these workers, many of the traditional assumptions about work, its organization, and its various meanings no longer hold true.

This segment of the work force, collectively referred to as the "contingent work force," is expanding. Part-time employment, for example, has been growing 10 percent faster than full-time employment since 1968 (9 to 5 1986, iii; U.S. House 1988, 6; U.S. Department of Labor, Women's Bureau, 1988). Part-time workers, voluntary and involuntary, comprised nearly a fifth of the U.S. work force in 1992 (U.S. Department of Commerce 1993, 402; see also Tilly 1989). And employee leasing, in which agencies, using the economies of scale of a large work force, provide workers with insurance and other benefits while "leasing" them to smaller companies, grew to more than fifteen hundred companies covering nearly a million workers from 1978 to 1988 (Day 1988, 59).[1] Though accurate aggregate figures are difficult to gather, estimates currently place the size of the contingent work force at between 17 and 25 percent of all U.S. employment (9 to 5 1986, 4; Harrison and Bluestone 1988, 45; Kilborn 1993; Sperry 1993; Lewin 1994).

My research explores one sector of this rapidly expanding contingent work force: temporary employment. Although a relatively new industry, temporary work has become firmly rooted in present-day American society and culture.[2] The U.S. Census Bureau, for instance, solicited prospective census workers for the 1990 census with a brochure proclaiming such work the "best temporary job in America" (U.S. Department of Commerce 1989a). Using a slightly different tack, the National Geographic Society (1990) appealed to its members to renew their subscriptions early to avoid the costs of "the service of many temporary employees." Additionally, temporary work and temporary workers have crossed over into popular culture. Major film, television, and stage productions have featured temporary workers as major or recurring characters.

Indeed, temporary employment is not only well known; it is one of the fastest-growing industries in the economy today (Carey and Hazelbaker 1986; 9 to 5 1986, 13; Kilborn 1993; Morrow 1993; Sperry 1993; Lewin 1994; Parker 1994). In the mid-1980s temporary employment accounted for one out of every thirteen new jobs and was projected to increase 5 percent annually, a rate higher than the 1.3 percent projected growth rate for all industries (Carey and Hazelbaker 1986; 9 to 5 1986, 12; U.S. House 1988, 86). These projections, however, turned out to be a huge underestimation. Between 1982 and 1993 temporary employment increased almost 250 percent, ten times faster than the rate for overall employment (Ansberry 1993; Morrow 1993, 40; Sperry 1993). In 1992 and 1993 temporary employment respectively accounted for an astounding 26 and 15 percent of all new jobs created nationally (Lewin 1994, A[12]).

Not only has the industry grown in size but the variety of placements available through temporary agencies has also dramatically increased. Today client companies can order temporary accountants, bank tellers, biologists, chemists, chauffeurs, computer programmers, designers, drafters, engineers, executives, gardeners, graphic artists, lab technicians, lawyers, lifeguards, nurses, and writers in addition to the traditional clerical categories such as data entry clerks, receptionists, secretaries, typists, and word processors.[3] Notwithstanding the extensive media attention technical, professional, and managerial temporaries have received (see Asinof 1988; Cohen 1988; Kirkpatrick 1988; Reibstein 1988; Feinstein 1989; Garson 1992; Impoco 1993), the clerical sector is still the largest segment of the industry, accounting in some estimates for upward of 80 percent of all temporary employment (Olesen and Katsuranis 1978; Gannon 1984; Howe 1986; Halcrow 1988; Harrison and Bluestone 1988; Parker 1994).

Despite their growing numbers, temporaries, like many contingent workers, are still considered to be on the fringes of the labor force and the society. Indeed, the marginality of temporaries can be seen in the various labels applied to this occupational group; "secondary," "peripheral," and "fringe" (Morse 1969; 9 to 5 1986; Kornbluh 1988; U.S. House 1988; Christensen 1991). These particular categorizations, with their semantic and symbolic weightings, are routinely used to deny temporary workers the legal access to social, political, and institutional protections granted full-time or permanent employees. Temporary workers, for example, rarely qualify for paid health plans, vacation pay, pension plans, or even unemployment insurance benefits. Like the unemployed (Newman

1988), temporary workers are socially marginalized and stigmatized. Temporaries, both on and off the job, have their personal commitments, qualifications, and integrity questioned.

Despite mounting evidence that the rapid growth in temporary employment has been driven more by employer than employee demand, the common assumption is that individual temporary workers prefer or choose temporary work or possess personal characteristics that account for their employment in the temporary sector. Industry claims of greater scheduling flexibility, varied and satisfying work experiences, skill acquisition and development, access to permanent employment opportunities, and a cornucopia of other supposed monetary and nonmonetary rewards, for example, are often accepted as valid and compelling, if unsupported, explanations for why individuals seek temporary employment. From this labor-supply perspective, changes in the character of the labor force—particularly increases in the number of working women and younger workers who presumably prefer and choose temporary work—have driven the recent spectacular growth of the temporary industry. Alternatively, temporaries are assumed to possess serious characterological flaws that prevent their employment in full-time, "real" jobs. Position in the occupational structure, then, is believed to reflect personal preference or individual qualifications.

Others, however, attribute the rapid growth in temporary employment to employer rather than employee demands (see Golden and Appelbaum 1992; Parker 1994). From this labor-demand perspective, employers are driving the growth of temporary work through reorganizing their corporate work forces into core and peripheral workers to decrease their labor costs. Since temporary workers can be hired for lower wages, without the payroll expenses of health care and other benefits, employers are creating contingent positions rather than full-time positions.

* * *

The account of temporary employment presented in the following chapters is not the standard laudatory perspective common in the popular press. It does not, for example, adopt the outlook of temporary industry leaders, corporate executives, or personnel managers or use a language of cost containment, profit margins, or efficiency. Instead, it is a look at temporary employment from the perspective of those who take the assignments, go from company to company, and do the work. Rather than focusing on labor costs, then, this study focuses on the costs to labor. What is the experience of working in the temporary employment sector?

The Temporary Help Service Industry

The temporary help industry consists of agencies that employ workers for rent or hire by other client companies for work assignments as short as half a day and as long as several months. Temporary agencies hire workers after skills testing and one-on-one interviews. Once workers have registered with the agency, their contact information is filed according to their skills and availability. Client companies contact the agency and place orders for temporary workers which detail the work tasks, duration of the assignment, working hours, and location. Agency "counselors" fill these orders by matching client company requests with an available and appropriately "skilled" temporary. Once a temporary accepts an assignment, she or he is generally given a job number, the company name and address, and the name of a contact person. The individual temporary worker goes to the client company on the appropriate day at the specified time and completes the assigned work for a prearranged hourly wage.

Typically, "rented" workers complete work for the client on the client company's premises, with its equipment, and under its supervision; on some occasions, however, the work is completed under the supervision of the agency, in the agency office, or even in the worker's home. The temporary agency bills the client company at an hourly rate for the work completed and pays the worker approximately 40 to 60 percent of this rate (Kirkpatrick 1988). Though agencies must withhold taxes, mandated social security, and worker's compensation and cover other overhead costs, substantial profits are made (Moore 1963; Joray 1972; Carey and Hazelbaker 1986; Harrison and Bluestone 1988; Doeringer 1991; Parker 1994).

Generally, "benefits" such as health insurance, vacation pay, sick leave, unemployment insurance, and other expenses associated with full-time, white-collar, and salaried employment are not provided temporary workers. Moreover, unable to meet the minimum earnings, minimum hours, or full-time "availability" requirements (in effect in forty-four states), most temporary workers are automatically excluded from unemployment insurance benefits (9 to 5 1986, iv). In addition, though temporaries with long tenure may be offered the opportunity to enroll in group health and life insurance through the agency, unlike full-time employees, temporaries frequently must pay 100 percent of their premiums. Consequently, enrollment in these plans is quite low. Indeed, these benefit plans may be more symbolic than functional, allowing the industry to appear concerned about temporary workers without actually having to make a financial commitment to provide benefits or services.

Although temporary agencies existed in the United States as early as 1920, the field's status as an industry is primarily a post–World War II phenomenon. Many of the current national industry leaders were established in the period immediately following the Second World War; Kelly Girls and Manpower, for example, were founded in 1947 and 1948, respectively (Moore 1963; Joray 1972; Gannon 1978; Hulin and Joray 1978). The temporary industry today is dominated by three large corporations: Manpower, Kelly, and Olsten.[4] Manpower, with company-owned and franchised offices in the United States and abroad, is the largest. In 1990 it had $3.5 billion in revenues. Kelly Services, with a primarily United States–based system of company-owned offices, is the second largest, with revenues of $1.4 billion in 1990. And Olsten Corporation, with both company-owned and franchised offices in the United States and Canada, had $838 million in revenues during 1990 (Berck 1992). Overall, annual receipts from firms supplying taxable temporary help increased from an estimated $9 million in 1985 to $19.2 million in 1990 (U.S. Department of Commerce 1989b, 785; U.S. Department of Labor 1991, 16).

The temporary help industry, unlike its "employees," is politically well organized (Cook 1994). The National Association of Temporary Services (NATS) and affiliated state associations promote the industry and monitor legislation (such as unemployment, worker's compensation, health care reform) that threatens to curtail the industry's growth and profits (Gonos 1992; Cook 1994). The California Association of Temporary Services (CATS), for example, employs a full-time lobbyist to monitor that state's employment legislation. Patricia Bepristis, the executive secretary of CATS, bluntly states, "[Our lobbyist] has the clout with the Senators and Congressmen so that when legislation comes up, we can get through to them. They remember the dollars. They remember that the association gave money to them" (Cook 1994, 126). The associations claim to represent the interests of their "employees" by protecting the industry. Dubiously equating their workers' interests with those of the temporary industry, they lobby against extending the benefits provided to full-time workers to temporary workers.

Not surprisingly, the number of people finding employment in the temporary sector has soared along with the tremendous expansion of the industry. In 1946 the handful of existing agencies employed only "a few thousand" people. Ten years later the figure was "about 20,000" people (Gannon 1978, 44). By 1983 the Bureau of Labor Statistics reported that there were nearly 472,000 temporary employees (U.S. Department of Labor 1992). Recently, employment growth in the industry has been even more dramatic. Indeed, in January 1993 the Bureau of Labor Statistics estimated that nearly 1.5 million workers, or 1.3 percent of the total work force, were employed through temporary agencies (Kilborn 1993, 6[A]; Sperry 1993, 1).

These figures, however, include only temporaries contracted directly through independent temporary employment agencies. An unknown number of temporary employees are hired directly by client companies from internal temporary pools, or "floater pools." In 1985 Cigna Corporation, for example, hired 60 percent of all temporary employees in its home office directly (9 to 5 1986, 13). As the cost of hiring temporary help has risen, many universities, law firms, and other large concerns have begun operating their own internal temporary services (Bassett 1989). A 1989 Conference Board survey, for instance, found that 49 percent of the 521 largest U.S. corporations examined had established internal temporary pools and an additional 9 percent were currently studying such a possibility. Although the number of temporary workers enrolled in any one internal pool has generally been small, collectively these pools may boost the overall number of temporary workers significantly (Christensen 1991).

The Temporary Work Force

Who are these workers? Early temporary agencies assumed from the beginning that temporary employment was "women's work." This assumption was reflected in the common inclusion of the word "girl" in the names of the newly formed temporary agencies (such as Kelly Girl, Western Girl, Right Girl). Recruitment efforts in the early industry specifically targeted and courted women. Women who worked as temporaries, however, were reminded that their participation should always be secondary to their primary feminine roles as wives and mothers. Temporary employment, with its intermittent work availability and without a promotional track, fit well with an existing national ideology that assumed that women's labor activity was transitory, impermanent, and secondary.

During the early 1960s, while Kelly Girl was inviting "housewives to meetings in suburban hotels to view films on the advantages of working," it was still "common policy" not to accept male applicants for clerical temporary work (Moore 1963, 35). In 1963 the president of Kelly Girls said, "We can think of 60,000 reasons why our 60,000 female employees want to work on a temporary basis, but we cannot think of one good reason why a man, other than a student or a man between jobs, would want to work as a temporary employee unless he wants to 'moonlight' " (Moore 1963, 29). Men, it was assumed, should be seeking permanent, full-time work—legitimate work that would facilitate taking on the idealized male role of the family provider. In recent years, however, these formal policies excluding men from temporary employment have been reversed.

Although temporary help firms have formally modernized their names (i.e., Kelly Girl became Kelly Services, Western Girl became Western Services, and Right Girl became Right Temporaries), they are still commonly referred to by their former monikers. These monikers may be objectionable because of their use of the infantilizing term "girl," but the gendered composition of the temporary work force they connote is not far from the mark. The clerical sector of temporary employment, like the general full-time clerical sector, is predominantly made up of women (Moore 1963; Gannon 1978; Olesen and Katsuranis 1978; McNally 1979; Howe 1986). Although more men have been seeking employment through temporary agencies (Olesen and Katsuranis 1978, 320), they still constitute a relatively small proportion of the clerical temporary work force.

In May 1985, for the first time, the Current Population Survey included questions about "workers who viewed their jobs as temporary and whose salaries were being paid by a temporary help supply agency" (Howe 1986, 45). At that time, women, who accounted for only two out of every five permanent (wage and salary) positions, accounted for nearly two-thirds of the temporary work force. Similarly, while only one out of every five permanent positions was held by a young worker (aged sixteen to twenty-four), one-third of all temporary positions were filled by young workers. Black workers were also disproportionately overrepresented in the temporary work force. Nearly twice the proportion of black workers present in other industries, or 20 percent of all temporary workers, were black.

Expansion, Scientific Management, and Feminization

The establishment and tremendous growth of the clerical temporary industry was made possible, at least in part, by the earlier expansion of the clerical employment sector generally. Large modern American corporations, at least as we know them today, began to emerge in the late nineteenth and early twentieth centuries (Mills 1956; Braverman 1974; Kanter 1977; Davies 1982; Fine 1990; Strom 1992). At the turn of the century the rapid consolidation and merging of many small and dispersed companies created huge new organizations. In 1901 more than 150 smaller firms consolidated to form the giant U.S. Steel Corporation, for example (Kanter 1977, 19). The period from 1897 to 1904 witnessed "more than four thousand firms merged into 257 combinations, trusts, or corporations" (Strom 1992, 17). These new corporate giants, along with significant expansions in the government sector and the growth of industries such as insurance, banking, and mail order houses, created an enormous demand for record-keeping, accounting, correspondence, and general communications personnel (Mills 1956; Braverman 1974; Davies 1982; Fine 1990; Strom 1992).

Consequently, the clerical occupational sector experienced dramatic growth in conjunction with the rise of the modern corporation (Mills 1956; Glenn and Feldberg 1982; Strom 1992). In 1880 only 4.3 percent, or 186,000, of all employed Americans held clerical positions (Glenn and Feldberg 1982, 204). In the decade between 1910 and 1920 alone, however, nearly three million new clerical positions were created (Strom 1992, 48). This growth, while large in absolute numbers, was also disproportionately large in comparison to the expansion of the industrial sector (Glenn and Feldberg 1982; Strom 1992). The ratio of manual workers to white-collar workers in manufacturing establishments, for example, declined from 11.4 in 1899 to only 5.8 in 1921 (Strom 1992, 48). By 1992 clerical positions comprised nearly 20 percent of the labor force (U.S. Department of Commerce 1993, 406).

Office work in the early twentieth century not only was expanding at an explosive rate, requiring substantial reorganization, but also was undergoing a dramatic transformation in terms of gender (Davies 1982; Hartmann 1982; Kessler-Harris 1982; Fine 1990; Goldin 1990; Strom 1992). Clerical work, which first appeared as a notable and separate occupational category in the United States in the nineteenth century, was initially an exclusively male field (Kessler-Harris 1982; Davies 1982; Strom 1992). The first women clerical workers were hired by the federal government during the Civil War (Strom 1982). Yet a decade later, in 1870, enumerators in New York City counted only five female shorthand writers (Kessler-Harris 1982). At the national level "less than one-half of 1 percent" of working women were employed as clerks, cashiers, typists, and stenographers (Kessler-Harris 1982, 407).[5] By 1900 2 percent of women workers were employed in these clerical jobs (Kessler-Harris 1982, 148). And by 1920 the ranks of women clerical workers (swelled by World War I) accounted for over 50 percent of all clerical positions (Hartmann 1982, 92–93; Kessler-Harris 1982, 148; Fine 1990; Goldin 1990). Women's presence in the clerical field continued to grow over the ensuing decades, and their predominance was soon firmly established. Clerical work, in a relatively short historical span, completely reversed its initial gender-typing as "men's work" to become female-dominated and identified as "women's work."

What produced this reversal? The rapid growth of women's labor force participation, particularly among married women, is one possible and frequently offered explanation. Whereas only 19 percent of all women had been engaged in wage labor in 1890, by 1910 over 25 percent of all women were employed outside the home (Chafe 1972, 55; Goldin 1990, 10). Among married women only 5 percent had been engaged in wage labor in 1890 (Goldin 1990, 10). Indeed, as late as 1939 the national expectation, sometimes codified or legislated, was for women to leave the labor force at the time of marriage (Goldin 1990, 13). But the barriers to married women's employment were falling, and the percentage of married women working for wages continued to grow. By 1992 nearly 60 percent of married women worked in the labor force (U.S. Department of Commerce 1993, 399). Yet changes in women's labor force participation rates alone, as dramatic as they have been, cannot adequately explain the concentration of women in clerical work.

Many scholars of work have argued that the feminization of clerical work occurred as the work was transformed from an exclusively male, relatively skilled, craftlike occupation in the nineteenth century to a semiskilled, proletarianized, low-status occupation in the twentieth (Mills 1956; Lockwood 1958; Braverman 1974; Glenn and Feldberg 1979; Davies 1982). Early-nineteenth-century clerical positions, from this perspective, were apprenticeships that required a great deal of overall knowledge of the organization and a wide variety of office and managerial skills and frequently led to career advancement or even the opening of one's own business (Lockwood 1958; Braverman 1974; Davies 1982; Glenn and Feldberg 1982; Fine 1990).

As corporations grew and the clerical occupations expanded, however, scientific management techniques—including highly detailed divisions of labor and the introduction of new office technologies[6]—fragmented and deskilled clerical work. The proletarianization thesis argues that tasks that had previously been the province of individual clerks were broken "into a series of steps, which were then reordered to save time, and/or divided among different groups of workers" (Glenn and Feldberg 1982, 204; see also Braverman 1974; Kanter 1977). Functionally distinct departments were created to handle limited and bounded work tasks in the largest corporations. As the "rationalization" of office work continued, many clerical workers were stripped of their worker-specific office knowledge and found themselves reassigned to the filing, stenography, billing, payroll, or various other single-detail and single-activity divisions (Braverman 1974; Kanter 1977; McNally 1979; Glenn and Feldberg 1982; Ferguson 1984). No longer engaged in a wide variety of tasks requiring diverse skills and personal judgment, many clerical workers instead attended to specific, isolated, and often mechanically regulated tasks:

> Typists, mail sorters, telephone operators, stock clerks, receptionists, payroll and timekeeping clerks, shipping and receiving clerks are subjected to routines, more or less mechanized according to current possibilities, that strip them of their former grasp of even a limited amount of office information, divest them of the need or ability to understand and decide, and make of them so many mechanical eyes, fingers, and voices whose functioning is, insofar as possible, predetermined by both rules and machinery. (Braverman 1974, 340)

Office work, consequently, was reorganized, rationalized, fragmented, deskilled, and proletarianized (Braverman 1974; Kanter 1977; Glenn and Feldberg 1979; Crompton and Reid 1982; Davies 1982; Glenn and Feldberg 1982; Machung 1983; Werneke 1984; Strom 1992).

The (re)organization of many clerical positions, with the assistance of the efficiency experts, along the same lines as manual factory labor led many analysts to note that the traditional distinctions between blue-collar and white-collar work were no longer applicable (Braverman

1974; Garson 1975; Kanter 1977; Davies 1982; Glenn and Feldberg 1982; Feldberg and Glenn 1983). Evelyn Nakano Glenn and Roslyn L. Feldberg, for example, note:

> The features that distinguish clerical work, justifying its inclusion among "middle-class" occupations, are: clean physical surroundings, an emphasis on mental as opposed to manual activities, reliance on workers' judgment in executing tasks, and direct personal contact among workers and between workers and managers. Proletarianization occurs as clerical work loses these special characteristics, i.e., as work is organized around manual rather than mental activities, as tasks become externally structured and controlled, and as relationships become depersonalized. (1982, 203)

While significant differences in the physical settings of office and manufacturing work persisted, differences in the organization of the work processes and the character of relations between management and labor, these analysts argue, narrowed.

Furthermore, as the status and skill level of office work declined, women, as a cheap, literate, and increasingly available source of labor, were hired into the office in large numbers (Braverman 1974; Davies 1982; Glenn and Feldberg 1982; Fine 1990).[7] Indeed, the rapidly increasing rate of women's labor force participation generally and a revolution in national gender ideologies, these analysts suggest, created the necessary conditions for the rapid feminization of clerical work (Davies 1982; Strom 1992). For example, restrictive social and legal barriers to women's employment, including the marriage bar and protective legislation limiting women's working hours, fell quickly in the wake of labor shortages created by World War I and World War II (Chafe 1972; Hartmann 1982; Kessler-Harris 1982; Goldin 1990; Strom 1992). Wartime labor shortages allowed women to enter traditional as well as nontraditional occupations in large numbers (Hartmann 1982). As one female banking executive during World War I observed, "It was not until our men were called overseas that we made any real onslaught on the realm of finance, and became tellers, managers of departments, and junior and senior officers" (quoted in Kessler-Harris 1982, 219).

Once women were employed, their competent work performance "challenged the physiological and social assumptions that justified discrimination against them" (Kessler-Harris 1982, 219; see also Chafe 1972; Hartmann 1982; Strom 1992). Nevertheless, many women hired into higher-pay manufacturing jobs during the world wars were summarily fired with the return of peacetime, while women clerical workers were frequently allowed to remain in the office (Hartmann 1982; Strom 1992).

Other scholars, however, contend that the proletarianization thesis overstates the extent to which clerical work has been deskilled (Cohn 1985). These theorists begin by arguing that the quality of clerical work in the nineteenth century has been greatly romanticized (Anderson 1976; Cohn 1985). Pointing to a substantial secondary strata of nineteenth-century clerical work, these scholars note that a great deal of "the work in early offices was done not by clerks but by copyists" (Anderson 1976; Cohn 1985, 67). The copyists were low-level employees, often boys, who handled much of the routine and tedious work in the office:

> Copyists were temporary workers, comparable to modern Kelly Girls, who were paid by the piece to do tasks involving writing. The work consisted of simple duties such as making copies of correspondence, addressing receipts, or making entries in ledgers. The job security, pay, and prospects of these positions was marginal. The skills required were negligible, since transcription requires few skills other than literacy and penmanship.
> (Cohn 1985, 67)

Rather than a homogeneous group of highly skilled male artisans, then, a much wider variety of (male) workers performed early office work. Gregory Anderson (1976), far from confirming that all full-time British clerks were highly skilled apprentices, documented high levels of unemployment, marginal employment, and poverty in his study of Victorian clerks.

These scholars, challenging the belief in an earlier "golden era" for clerks, argue that it is not at all clear that clerical work was deskilled by the introduction of new office technologies (Cohn 1985). Indeed, new technologies may have increased the skill levels required in certain clerical occupations as some lower-level, routine tasks were automated or eliminated. Rather than static skill requirements that are chipped away little by little with every new technological or organizational innovation, skill requirements in clerical work have been more mutable, changing as the work is reorganized and recombined into various clerical occupations.

Furthermore, these scholars argue that the proletarianization thesis cannot adequately explain the feminization of clerical labor. Samuel Cohn (1985), for example, argues that clerical work first became feminized in industries and firms that were clerical labor intensive and could not afford to "prefer" more expensive male labor. Since women were generally paid less, the costs to employers of hiring women were considerably lower. As the Librarian of Congress said of women workers in 1870, "they could give good service for less pay than the men on his staff, thus resulting in economy" (quoted in Strom 1992, 177). Additionally, whereas men might continue to work for years, earning substantial increases in pay, women's tenure could be "legitimately" manipulated through the marriage bar to hold down costs. As Cohn argues, "hiring sixteen-year-old women and forcing them to retire at marriage ensures careers anywhere from six to ten years long. This is long enough to ensure the conservation of any firm-specific skills, but not so long as to create a severe crisis of productivity" (Cohn 1985, 225). Women were also available for work in large numbers, while other groups of secondary labor were becoming more scarce (for example, as the supply of boys decreased with the passage of child labor and mandatory schooling laws).

The Limits of Routinization

Both perspectives fail to account adequately for the diversity and variability of skill requirements within clerical work as a whole (for example, the work of a data entry clerk, word processor, and an executive secretary, though all requiring typing, are not equivalent).

Rather than a homogeneous occupational sector that has been completely and uniformly fragmented, deskilled, and proletarianized or one that has been reskilled or upgraded, clerical work is composed of positions that are extremely rationalized and routine as well as those that are nonrationalized and varied.

Harry Braverman, observing dramatic efforts in the early 1970s to bring an end to the "social office," assumed that all clerical work that had not already been subdivided, fragmented, and deskilled soon would be. As he watched, scientific management, through the establishment of word processing and administrative centers, appeared poised to subdivide and fragment the entire clerical occupational sector, even those secretarial positions that had remained more varied and challenging:

> From the beginning, office managers held that all forms of clerical work, not just routine or repetitive ones, could be standardized and "rationalized." For this purpose they undertook elaborate studies of even those occupations which involved little routine, scores of different operations each day, and the exercise of judgment. The essential feature of this effort was to make the clerical worker, of whatever sort, account for the entire working day. Its effect was to make the work of every office employee, no matter how experienced, the subject of management interference. (Braverman 1974, 309)

Indeed, Braverman believed that once this process began, it would advance rapidly. Because clerical work was unencumbered by the physical limitations of moving heavy industrial materials, being "conducted almost entirely on paper," he envisioned few bulwarks against the efficiency experts and their reorganization of the office: "In general, the rationalization of most office work and the replacement of the all-around clerical worker by the subdivided detail worker proceeds easily because of the nature of the process itself" (Braverman 1974, 315).

But as Sharon Hartman Strom has argued in her history of office work, "only so many [office] jobs could be routinized" (1992, 174). As other clerical positions were rationalized, tasks that proved difficult to systemize were bundled into the jobs of secretaries. These more varied jobs, then, became the repository for tasks that had resisted the earlier efforts of scientific management—perhaps inoculating them against future attempts at rationalization. Furthermore, not everyone in the office responded passively to the efforts of the efficiency experts. Strom contends that "both employers and workers resisted the penetration of rationalization too far up the office hierarchy or too far into men's work" (1992, 174). Both secretaries and their bosses (who faced the loss of an important source of symbolic status as well as personalized attention and assistance), for example, opposed efforts to abolish the historically privileged secretary-boss relationship.

The organization of clerical work that emerged from these rationalization efforts, then, was still a two-tiered system. The distinctions that had prevailed between clerks and copyists in the nineteenth century (Cohn 1985) and between secretaries and stenographers in the early twentieth century (Strom 1992) were retained. Rosabeth Moss Kanter (1977), in her examination of the corporation, describes this dual system of clerical work in operation:

> Secretarial work was divided into two kinds: marriage-like and factory-like. The elite corps of private secretaries were directly attached to one or more bosses for whom they did a variety of tasks and from whom they derived status. Other secretarial work was done in steno and typing pools whose occupants were little more than extensions of their machines—and highly replaceable at that. (Kanter 1977, 27)

The overall impact of scientific management was to increase the number of routine or factory-like clerical positions, while maintaining at least a portion of marriage-like and more varied secretarial jobs.[8]

Temporary workers experience their work life within this highly bifurcated system. More often than not, temporaries possessing the required combination of minimal "skills"—computer literacy, typing, shorthand, or phone manner—are assigned to the routine, factory-like clerical work assignments (data entry, filing, photocopying, envelope stuffing, and the like). Indeed, it is this vision of increasingly routine clerical work, the relative insignificance of a training period, and the general inter-changeability of workers that the temporary clerical industry both fosters through their marketing efforts and serves (see Parker 1994).

Temporary workers are still occasionally assigned to marriage-like sec-retarial positions, however, where the work is more varied. Yet these positions are generally available only on a fill-in or replacement basis (that is, when a full-time employee is absent or unavailable). Addi-tionally, these fill-in, replacement, or coverage positions appear to con-stitute a much smaller proportion of today's temporary assignments. In a 1989 survey (Christensen 1991), for example, 81 percent of temporary agency hires and 83 percent of internal temporary pool hires were em-ployed exclusively for routine clerical and administrative support tasks.

The Growth of Contingent Employment

Why did temporary employment, after continuous but steady growth for a period of fifty years, expand so rapidly and dispro-portionately in the last two decades? Ultimately, to answer this question, we must turn to an examination of changes in the very structure of the U.S. economy.

U.S. workers and their employers enjoyed an unprecedented expand-ing economy in the twenty-year period immediately after World War II (Harrison and Bluestone 1988). Average family incomes and corporate profits were both on the rise. More workers expected, and received, benefits such as health insurance, pension plans, training, and paid vaca-tions from their employers. And new generations of workers could gen-uinely expect to be better off than their parents (Harrison and Bluestone 1988). But changes in the global economy were brewing that would eventually threaten this prosperity and sense of national well-being.

U.S.-based corporations began to feel the effects of global competition and stagnating profits in the mid-1970s (Harrison and Bluestone 1988, 7; Doeringer 1991, 1). Net after-tax profit rates of domestic nonfinancial corporations, for instance, peaked at 10 percent in 1965 and then dropped to less than 6 percent a decade later (Harrison and Bluestone 1988, 7). This already painful corporate "profit squeeze" became excruciating in the early 1970s when the costs of production increased significantly. OPEC oil price hikes, government regulations, taxes, inflation, and the rising cost of employee wages and benefits all cut deeper into corporate America's bottom line (Bluestone and Harrison 1982; Bowles, Gordon, and Weisskopf 1983; Freedman 1985; Harrison and Bluestone 1988; Doeringer 1991).

U.S. corporations, faced with the possibility of further declines in profits and dissatisfied stockholders, knew that something had to be done to revive their bottom line. Management teams essentially had two choices for buoying up their sagging profit margins: significantly improve the quality of their products and productivity through new technology and organizational innovation or produce the same products "cheaper" by attacking and beating back the cost side of the equation (Harrison and Bluestone 1988, 12). American corporations chose to attack costs, particularly labor costs. Between 1980 and 1987 downsizing, outsourcing, mergers, and acquisitions activity among the Fortune 500 companies under the rubric of "restructuring" eliminated 3.1 million jobs (Doeringer 1991, 140; see also Newman 1988). And although many of these cutbacks were initially attributed to the recession, as the economy "recovered" in the early 1990s, it became clear that there would be no callbacks: U.S. corporations had entered a new period of being "lean and mean." Indeed, corporations have continued to shed jobs by the thousands, announcing new layoffs even while earning substantial profits. In 1993 more than 615,000 jobs were eliminated and economists were predicting even larger job losses for 1994 (Uchitelle 1994, 4[C]).

Besides outright labor force reductions, in some industries management successfully bargained for "givebacks" with labor—promising to avoid layoffs or plant closings for concessions in wage rates, benefit packages, or work rules and regulations (Katz 1985; Slaughter 1986; Bensman and Lynch 1987; Blin 1987; Harrison and Bluestone 1988; Bernstein 1992; Greenhouse 1992). And corporate America, with the initial symbolic nod of assent from Ronald Reagan's conservative National Labor Relations Board and the perfunctory firing of the nation's striking air traffic controllers (PATCO) in the early 1980s, began openly engaging in union busting (Harrison and Bluestone 1988, 102). Management had chosen a strategy, a strategy that President Richard Nixon's assistant secretary of labor, Arnold Weber, called "zapping labor" (Harrison and Bluestone 1988, 25). The post–World War II social contract around work and the American dream had begun to unravel.

The promise of full-time work and advancement through "internal labor markets," almost normative forms of post–World War II work organization (Doeringer and Piore 1971), started to become the province of only a small core of the U.S. work force. Beginning in the early 1970s, corporations began to organize their work forces on a core and periphery basis (Berger and Piore 1980; Piore and Sabel 1984; Mangum, Mayall, and Nelson 1985; 9 to 5 1986; Belous 1989a; Doeringer 1991). Core workers, those who could anticipate "a future with the company and for whom the company is willing to provide health insurance and retirement benefits," were first reduced and then held to a minimum (Eileen Appelbaum, quoted in 9 to 5 1986, 1). Corporate managers, lawyers, professionals, and other workers whose activities were deemed essential to the daily running of global corporations fill this upper tier of the new labor force (Bluestone and Harrison 1982; Harrison and Bluestone 1988; 9 to 5 1986). The lower tier is composed of peripheral workers, those who not only provide personal and business services to the upper tier but also act as a buffer to the core, absorbing economic fluctuations and cyclical downturns (9 to 5 1986; Harrison and Bluestone 1988; Waller 1989).[9] Peripheral workers, unlike core workers, generally do not have employer-provided benefits, have lower average wages, and experience greater variability in work hours (Bluestone and Harrison 1982; 9 to 5 1986; U.S. Department of Labor, 1988; Bureau of Labor Statistics, U.S. House 1988; Doeringer 1991). As Eileen Appelbaum noted, "Internal labor markets play a special role in meeting the needs of companies that are poised for expansion. . . . Today, however, companies are poised for contraction" (quoted in Harrison and Bluestone 1988, 45).

Throughout this restructuring, however, Reagan-Bush–era economists and supporters contended that the U.S. economy was producing plenty of new jobs as it shifted from a production base to a service base (Kutscher and Personik 1986; Brock 1987; Norwood 1987; Shelp 1987). Janet Norwood, then commissioner of the Bureau of Labor Statistics, argued that the lack of economic progress was due to "cyclical patterns" and to the 1981-82 recession "rather than a general inability of our economy to generate good jobs" (Norwood 1987). But others contend that the "Great American Jobs Machine" was producing jobs that were, well, less than great (Bluestone and Harrison 1982; Bensman and Lynch 1987; Cohen and Zysman 1987; Harrison and Bluestone 1988). As Bennett Harrison and Barry Bluestone have argued, "The reality of the new service economy entails a great many low-paying jobs and a much smaller layer of high-paying ones" (1988, 72). Indeed, between 1979 and 1984 nearly three out of five of the new jobs created, or 58 percent of all net new jobs, paid $7,400 or less a year in 1984 dollars (Harrison and Bluestone 1988, ix).

Even in postrecession 1992 a disproportionate number of new private sector jobs (about two-thirds) were temporary or part-time (Ansberry 1993, 1[A]). As Audrey Freedman notes, "The labor market today, if you look at it closely, provides almost no long-term secure jobs. It's a market in motion" (quoted in Kilborn 1993, 1[A]). For the displaced worker, the part-time job without health care coverage hardly qualified as a great or even comparable replacement job (see Bensman and Lynch 1987; Newman 1988, 1993).

Additionally, management, as part of its new labor cost containment campaign, began bringing in larger numbers of workers from outside the corporation, workers to whom they had few legal obligations.[10] Contingent workers (temporary, part-time, self-employed, and leased employees) could be hired on an hourly or piece-rate basis without the significant costs of employer-sponsored benefits. Moreover, these workers could be let go when the work was completed or business was slow. The short-term benefits to management were clear: cost savings through reducing both idle time and employee overhead costs such as payroll, health care insurance, unemployment, vacation, and sick leave (U.S.

House 1988; Doeringer 1991). It is estimated that contingent workers are 20 to 40 percent less expensive to employ than full-time core workers (Ansberry 1993, 1[A]).

Many analysts point to the rising costs of hiring workers directly as the driving force behind growth in contingent labor (Moore 1963; Olesen and Katsuranis 1978; Leone and Burke 1976; Gannon 1978; Hulin and Joray 1978; Tilly 1989; Christensen 1991; Golden and Appelbaum 1992). The costs of advertising, interviewing, pre-employment medical exams, and payroll processing for one full-time secretary, for example, amounted to several hundred dollars as early as the late 1970s (Hulin and Joray 1978, 261). In addition, the costs of fringe benefits typically provided to full-time workers but not contingent workers have risen dramatically. From 1915 (when worker's compensation laws were first introduced) to 1992, fringe benefits have increased to account for more than a third of the total cost of worker compensation (Joray 1972, 46; 9 to 5 1986, 21; Wiatrowski 1990, 29). Health care costs alone rose 12.1 percent, about four times as fast as the general cost of living, in 1991. Nationally, the average cost for employers of covering a single employee's health care in 1991 rose to $3,605 (Freudenheim 1992).

Indeed, the short-term benefits of hiring contingent workers prompted some employers to lay off and hire back all or substantial portions of their work force as less expensive, less protected contingent workers. A Massachusetts hospital, for example, laid off all licensed practical nurses and then hired them back as less expensive part-time workers with reduced benefits (9 to 5 1986, 41). Mellon Bank in Pittsburgh fired a unionized janitorial contractor, then hired the janitors back as part-time workers with no benefits (9 to 5 1986, 41). Other companies laid off full-time workers on one day and hired them back the next through an employee leasing agency that purported to provide health benefits but in fact did not (Helliker 1991; see also Feldman 1990). Warner-Lambert, as part of its corporate "restructuring program," laid off the full-time clerical staff of its New Jersey office and then hired some of the employees back as contingent workers through its newly created Temporary Secretarial Department (Creative downsizing 1992). And in a particularly egregious case, production workers laid off from General Electric in Morristown,

Tennessee (two weeks after the loss of a major union battle), were referred by the local unemployment office, under the Joint Partnership Training Act (JPTA),[11] to temporary agencies that then rented the workers back to General Electric at half the pay, no benefits, and with the payment of government "training" subsidies (Gonos 1992). To add injury to insult, "the workers found themselves being 'rolled over' every fifty-nine days—laid off for a couple of days and then rehired in the same job, so the company could keep them as temps and continue to collect the Government [training] subsidies" (Gonos 1992, 15).

Management teams in other corporations rushed to fill new-hire positions with cheaper contingent workers. In the 1980s the management of Wisconsin Physicians Services Insurance Corporation, for example, whose in-house, full-time work staff was unionized, pursued a strategy of hiring nonunionized, part-time homeworkers as insurance claims adjusters (Costello 1989). And at the University of Cincinnati departmental hiring officials were encouraged, "Break the tradition and cash in today!!" "What about two part-timers instead of one full-time employee?" they were asked (administration flyer quoted in 9 to 5 1986, iii).

Although the use of part-time workers for contingent staffing is still the most prevalent choice, the use of temporary employees is a close second (Tilly 1989; Christensen 1991, 143). Consequently, temporary employment also increased dramatically during the last two decades as businesses transformed their use of temporary employment from a fill-in, crisis management, or special project form of staffing to a permanent, routinized, budgetary staffing option (see Simonetti, Nykodym, and Sell 1988; Grossman and Magnus 1989; Parker 1994). Many temporary service agencies, recognizing the cost appeal of contingent workers, directly marketed their services to client companies through the claims of labor cost reductions in fringe benefits, training, and payroll. "You have better things to do than worry about employee payroll and benefits," trumpeted one agency's ad. Another simply read, "Norell's innovative solutions are now helping over 23,000 American companies use temporary staffing as a profitable management tool" (Crain's Directory of Temporary Services 1990, 62–63). Businesses responded to these appeals. A small California manufacturing firm, for example, said that using temporaries "saves time interviewing, there's no recruiting costs, no benefits to pay, and we're not responsible for unemployment costs" (Halcrow 1988).

In some cases today "temporary worker" is nothing more than an empty appellation with little or no connection to the actual job content or duration of the employment period. In Los Angeles one out of every six county workers is classified as temporary even though some of them have worked the same job for twenty years or more (U.S. House 1988, 42). In a case described in 1988, Violet Antonson had worked at the same Los Angeles County Public Library branch since 1957. In thirty years of temporary service she had never received employer-provided health insurance or paid vacations or made more than $5.42 an hour (Kirkpatrick 1988, 116). In January 1985, under the Reagan administration, federal civil service regulations were relaxed to allow government workers to be hired as temporary for up to four years without fringe benefits (Christensen 1987, 18; U.S. House 1988, 58). In January 1986 the Office of Personnel Management categorized three hundred thousand federal employees, including some postal workers, as temporary (Christensen 1987, 18). In such cases these classifications have little real meaning. They do, however, allow a semantic and legal justification (these workers do not fit the legally determined definition of an "employee") for differential wage and benefit payments (U.S. House 1988, 42). Though two government-commissioned studies recommended that federal temporary workers be provided with health benefits, the advice was rejected as too costly (9 to 5 1986, 22).

The temporary industry is still doing fill-in or replacement business, but the use of temporaries in assignments of several months or more as a labor cost management tool appears to be making up a growing share of the industry's receipts. Notwithstanding Manpower's slightly disingenuous claim that less than 2 percent of its work force is "assigned to a single customer for 1,500 hours per year or more," more management teams are creating permanent temporary positions in their staffing plans (U.S. House 1988, 99).[12] Thus although it may be true that no single temporary employee works more than 1,500 hours per year in any particular position, at least some positions that would otherwise be full-time are nominally temporary and filled by a succession of temporary workers. In 1988 surveys conducted by the National Association of Temporary Services and *Personnel Journal,* it was found that 25 and 21 percent of respondents, respectively, increased their use of temporaries to compensate for staff cuts and as a cost-effective alternative to hiring "regular employees" (Halcrow 1988). Between 1985 and 1988, for instance, Apple Computer increased its contracting of temporaries from 2 percent to nearly 17 percent of its work force (Kirkpatrick 1988). Ultimately, the engine driving the recent dramatic growth in temporary employment may be the cost differential for employers between hiring full-time and temporary employees.

2 Getting into It

Welcome to The Right Temporaries world. . . . Thousands of people who are unable to work in full-time or permanent work have found that the answer for them is to work in the temporary service field. . . . This may be your first venture into the business world . . . or you may be returning to business after an absence of many years. Perhaps you are between jobs, not certain what you really want . . . or maybe you have decided that you need extra income for your family. Whatever your status, you have taken a step in the right direction. (Right Temporaries, Inc., *Welcome to Right Temporaries, Inc.*)

In the temporary industry's literature the typical temporary is young, white, and female.[1] These women are portrayed as "choosing" to work as temporaries for nonessential economic reasons—luxury goods, diversionary activity, and "walking around" money. Such images, however, seriously distort, underrate, and obscure the economic constraints and needs behind most (female and male) workers' involvement in temporary employment.

One such distortion, what I call the "devoted mom" genre, depicts a woman, presumably attached to a male "breadwinner," who works as a temporary to earn a little "extra" income. "Cheryl needs a job that is flexible so she can pick her kids up from school every day and be home during vacations. Her counselor is careful to schedule Cheryl's assignments around her children's vacations and sends her to jobs located near the school" (Right Temporaries, Inc., Fall 1991, 2). Her place in the home as a wife and mother, not her work, is the core of this woman's identity. Her temporary work, in this imagery, is an extension of her familial or nurturing role—she does it as a sacrifice for her loved ones. And although temporary work pays less than other forms of employment, she is advised to remember that the tradeoff allows her to live up to her commitments to home and family.

Another popular characterization in the industry's literature is that of a "gregarious grandma." In this construction older women choose to work as temporaries not for economic reasons but for recreation or diversion:

> Sylvia, though retired, isn't the rocking chair type! She likes getting out, meeting new people and doing work that is worthwhile. But she also likes to take spur-of-the-moment trips with her husband. Her temporary counselor calls on Sylvia only for short-term assignments, knowing it's hard to keep Sylvia pinned down for long! (Right Temporaries, Inc., Fall 1991, 2).

These women are presented as older, "empty nest" versions of devoted moms.

Ubiquitous, too, in the industry literature is the image of the "chipper co-ed." Although most agencies have begun using the more gender-neutral construction "college student" in their promotional materials, when specific examples are given they are almost always female: "Martha needed summer employment to earn money for school. . . . Martha earned top dollar this summer, plus received valuable work experience and an impressive résumé!" (Right Temporaries, Inc., Fall 1991, 2). This typical temp is a seasonal worker, seeking temporary work only during school breaks. Like other temporary workers portrayed in the industry literature, her economic needs are met elsewhere; she seeks employment for pocket money only.[2] The college student's financial concerns, for example, are frequently trivialized: "Many prime assignments go to temps who would rather earn extra money than get a tan before hitting campus!" (Right Temporaries, Inc., Fall 1991, 5).

These promotional images perpetuate the myth that women's health and other essential economic needs are met through "family wage and benefits" packages (Barrett and McIntosh 1980, 50) accessed through connections to primary male wage earners—fathers and husbands. Historically, the assumption that "women workers were already well supported and sought a paying job only as a means of securing extra cash to indulge frivolous feminine desires" has allowed employers, politicians, and labor leaders alike to treat women as secondary and therefore marginal: paying them lower wages, providing few if any benefits or advancement opportunities, and generally ignoring their grievances (Chafe 1972, 62; Westwood 1984; Goldin 1990). The temporary industry's promotional images, like earlier "pin money" theories, are based on the serious misinterpretation, or the blatant denial, of the economic imperatives behind most women's employment.

Celluloid and Greasepaint Images

Popular culture provides two additional images of the typical temp: the "vixen" and the "ditz." The temporary secretary as "sexually available vixen" appeared in film and on stage in the late eighties and early nineties. For example, early in Spike Lee's 1990 film *Jungle Fever,* Angela, a temporary secretary, sleeps with her co-worker and supervisor on an assignment. Any portrayal of Angela's work life mysteriously disappears after this liaison. David Mamet's play *Speed-the-Plow* pursues this same theme of sexual availability when two movie executives bet on whether one of them can get the temporary secretary, played on Broadway by pop star Madonna, to deal with him "in any other than a professional way" (Mamet 1988, 37). In an even more unflattering appearance, the 1993 office horror-thriller *The Temp* portrays the title character, Kris, as a power-hungry, off-kilter temporary who uses her sexuality to get ahead. This character is so driven by the thirst for power that she will stop at nothing, including sabotage and murder, to get what she wants.

The "ditzy temporary," virtually a stock comic television character, put in a number of guest appearances during the eighties and nineties. In a minor subplot on a 1991 "L.A. Law" episode, for example, a temporary secretary hired at the firm manages to bungle every task she is assigned. Distraught with her own incompetence at work and in life generally, she climbs out onto a window ledge and threatens to jump to her death. Similarly, the incompetence of an endless string of temporary secretaries hired by Candice Bergen's character on "Murphy Brown" became one of the television series' most recognized running jokes. These images, while different from those produced by the temporary industry, also belittle and obscure the pressing economic motivation behind temporary workers' employment.

Economic Man, Irrational Woman

Many economists and other academic analysts leave these cultural assumptions unchallenged. Most analysts, for example, seem to dismiss or subordinate economic needs and labor market constraints as viable explanations for working as a temporary, seeking "preferences" and "motivations" in the character of individual workers instead. Implicit in these neoclassical analyses is the assumption that temporaries, as "economic men," are rational autonomous actors maximizing their personal preferences. Any individual's location in the temporary employment sector, then, is either a voluntary choice and a statement of personal preferences or a reflection of personal or characterological flaws.

Some scholars argue that at least a portion of the temporary work force is between jobs and actively seeking more permanent employment (Moore 1963; Gannon and Brainin 1971; Barrier 1989). Indeed, Mack A. Moore made a distinction between these "involuntarily displaced members of the labor force" and other "bona fide members" of the temporary work force (1963, 8). Similarly, Martin J. Gannon and Uri Brainin (1971, 172), in a study of employee tenure in the temporary industry, claim that temporaries who were rated "excellent" on "manner, voice, and grooming" were promptly hired out of the temporary employment sector and into permanent positions.

Alternatively, these analysts see longer-term involvement in temporary employment as a reflection of flaws in personality or character. Like the "ditz" of popular culture, many temporaries are assumed to share a set of characteristics, usually not very flattering ones, that make them unemployable or incapable of working on a permanent or full-time basis (Moore 1963; Gannon and Brainin 1971). Moore, for example, argued that "It is common knowledge that there are other workers who would not be as employable as direct applicants as they are as [temporary help supply] workers" (1963, 141). And Gannon and Brainin similarly maintained that "the temporary help industry may be providing a haven for those less attractive workers who would find difficulty in successfully negotiating the rigorous hiring procedure of established firms seeking a permanent work force" (1971, 172–73).

Other analysts have argued that temporaries constitute a unique new category of workers that simply prefer or choose noncommittal work over permanent employment. Gannon, for example, supported this voluntaristic framework in a national study of temporary health care workers. He found that, when asked to select the "most important reason for choosing to work for [their temporary] firm," the majority (60 percent) chose an item that read "freedom to schedule my work in a flexible manner" (Gannon 1984). Similarly, Wayne Howe (1986) of the Bureau of Labor Statistics argues that if there is a disproportionate number of women working as temporaries, it must be because women have a preference for temporary employment. The ratio of women in temporary as opposed to permanent work, according to Howe, "clearly reflects the benefits offered to many women by the temporary help supply service industry" (1986, 46). He offers a similar explanation for the disproportionate number of young workers.[3]

Temporary Narratives, or "Getting into It"

The "getting into it" narratives from my interviews challenge the applicability of this framework of choice, voluntarism, and character. These stories allow an in-depth examination of personal preferences, structural constraints, and their intersections for a limited yet instructive number of cases. "How or when did you first start working as a temporary?" elicited straightforward narratives about the circumstances and events leading individuals to begin temporary employment.

These narratives often contradicted the routinized, ex post facto responses, reconciling personal behavior and circumstance with preference, regularly offered to direct questions of personal motivation. When asked, for example, "Why did you start temping?" or "What was the best thing about working as a temporary?" temporaries almost invariably responded with rote explanations about the flexibility of scheduling.[4] Yet when I pursued such statements, they often seemed hollow. The same people who cited flexibility as a motivating factor complained about the unpredictable supply of work and never refused a proffered assignment or quit a particularly unpleasant one.

One temporary, Helen, catching herself about to expound on the virtues of flexibility, compared her response to the automatic, even robotic, behavior of Ira Levin's suburban housewife characters in the *Stepford Wives*:

> KH: Is there anything that you think is the best thing about working temp?
>
> H: Well, I would say flexibility, but I haven't taken advantage of that at all. Wow. Subliminal marketing. *Stepford Wives*. Stepford Temps, right? Robots. So flexibility really isn't the best part.

Marketing, yes; subliminal, not necessarily. Advertising, registration, and other materials produced by the temporary industry, along with cultural images, often tout flexibility as a benefit of temporary employment to prospective and current temporary workers. Not surprisingly, temporaries often cite it to others, whether or not it conforms to their experience, when explaining and justifying their involvement in temporary employment.

Transitionals

Many who join the ranks of the temporary work force define their involvement as an in-between, stop-gap, or transitional measure. These self-defined transitional temporaries are actively seeking permanent positions often within the same companies or industries in which they work on a temporary basis. Transitional temporaries are often recently displaced workers (voluntary and involuntary), displaced homemakers, and recent college graduates. Seeking entry or reentry positions into the full-time labor force, these individuals pursue clerical temporary employment as a last-resort income source as well as a job-seeking strategy.

Transitional temporaries appear to make up a large segment of the temporary work force at any particular point in time. Dick Gorman, vice-president of Flexi-Force in Milwaukee, for example, estimated that 75 to 80 percent of his company's temporaries were looking for full-time work (9 to 5 1986, iv). Agency counselors in my study believed 50 to 70 percent of their temporary employees were seeking full-time employment. Indeed, acceptance of a permanent position is the major reason cited for the high turnover in the temporary industry (Gannon and Brainin 1971; U.S. House 1988, 95). It seems clear that a large proportion, if not the majority, of temporaries accept temporary employment as a transitional measure rather than as a permanent employment choice (see also Parker 1994).

Downsizing Refugee Seeks Permanent Position

Laid-off and other involuntarily displaced workers often find their way to the temporary industry's payroll (see Newman 1988). A variety of factors contributed to a large pool of involuntarily displaced workers in the late eighties and early nineties. In Chicago the unemployment rate reached a high of 10.3 percent in December 1991—3.2 percent above the national unemployment rate (Wilkerson 1992, 1 [A]). The city's unemployment problems were dramatically spotlighted in the national news when more than nine thousand people stood in subzero temperatures, some for as long as twelve hours, to apply for five hundred primarily low-wage service jobs at a new hotel (Wilkerson 1992).

The national media were quick to point out that a disproportionate share of the jobs lost in the late eighties and early nineties were in traditionally recession-resistant white-collar occupations. *Newsweek*, for example, noted that in 1990 fully a third of unemployed workers were white-collar (Schwartz et al. 1990, 47). And journalistic reports rarely failed to mention the mix of younger, college-educated people waiting in lines at unemployment offices, noting how highly skilled and well-paid employees had fallen so far that they were now working at the very bottom of the American job market—in the temporary employment sector. For instance, *Newsweek* described the case of "a former banker who speaks five languages and is now working as a temp" (Schwartz et al. 1990, 47).

Mike was one of the involuntarily displaced workers. He was employed at a large bank in the Northeast when the recession arrived in the late eighties. He had been working for the same company for nearly four years and felt relatively secure in his job. During that time he had moved from being a teller, to a position in the credit department and eventually into the cash management department. But when the bank hit hard times, it contracted, first moving him to another, less prestigious department and finally eliminating his position entirely. "They said, 'Sorry, we can't have your job anymore.' But you never expect that sort of thing. You think, 'I'm here forever.'" At first Mike continued to look for full-time work in the Northeast, surviving on unemployment insurance and an occasional singing engagement. Eventually, with his resources almost depleted, he moved to the Chicago area to live with his father and stepmother until he could "get back on [his] feet."

Initially, Mike attempted to find employment in the Chicago banking industry comparable to his previous experience and position in the Northeast. But in a city in which banking positions were contracting rather than expanding (shortly after our interview, for example, one of Chicago's largest banks announced another substantial layoff [Pae 1991]), his efforts appeared futile. With the encouragement of his stepmother, Mike decided to register for temporary employment:

> I didn't even think of temping as an option at first. I just frantically sent out résumés. And got very nice rejection letters in return. Finally, my stepmother suggested that I do some temp work. And I thought, "Oh my God. I'm very above this. Why would I ever want to be a temp?" But after about a month of sitting at home watching Oprah and the soaps and thinking too much, I thought that I'd better do something. So I called a couple of places, but Busy Temps was the only place that wanted to see me immediately. And when I went there they gave me all the tests and everything. I had an assignment the next day.

Mike did not, however, abandon his hopes of finding a permanent position. In fact, he pursued temporary assignments in banking, hoping to use them as an entrée to a full-time position in Chicago's banking industry. For Mike, and for others purged involuntarily from permanent payrolls in the late eighties and early nineties, temporary employment seemed better than no work at all (see Newman 1988).

New Graduate Seeks Permanent Position

Many private and public college students, confronted with a scarcity of desirable employment options on graduation in the late eighties and early nineties (see Gose 1994; Kilborn 1994), also entered the temporary employment sector as a last-resort or transitional survival measure—"Just until I can find full-time, permanent employment." Indeed, between 1989 and 1992 entry-level positions for college graduates declined by almost one-third (Hinds 1992). Northwestern University's Lindquist-Endicott Report found in 1992 that half of all businesses surveyed intended to hire fewer new college graduates (Hinds 1992).

Victor R. Lindquist, one of the authors of this study, remarked of the current employment situation, "This is worse than anything I've seen in twenty years" (Hinds 1992, 1[A]). Echoing this tone of pessimism, a Michigan State University study found that 42 percent of the 1.1 million expected 1992 graduates were earning degrees in the social sciences and other areas already oversupplied with candidates (Hinds 1992). During this same period, 1989 to 1991, pay for college-educated people unexpectedly lagged behind the rate of inflation. A college degree, commanding an adjusted average of $17.55 an hour in the late 1980s, had declined to an adjusted average of $16.69 an hour in 1991 (Uchitelle 1992).

As the value of a bachelor's degree declined and the job market produced fewer "good jobs," more college graduates lowered their expectations, accepting chronic underemployment in order to survive. For example, between 1990 and 1993 the percentage of new graduates from the University of Toledo taking contingent jobs on graduation grew from approximately 10 percent to 30 percent (Kilborn 1993, 6[A]). As Janet Norwood, former commissioner of the Labor Department's Bureau of Labor Statistics and a senior fellow at the Urban Institute, noted, "The college-educated can at least go down, but the people below them have nowhere to go" (quoted in Uchitelle 1992, 1[A]). Temporary work, though it is low-status and may not fully use their hard-earned college skills, is one way for recent graduates to survive and save face while continuing to seek a more satisfying and socially valued position in the primary labor market.

Bob, for example, a graduate of a private midwestern university, was certain that his good grades and internship experience would lead to a permanent position. But when graduation came, he was still unemployed:

> When I graduated I didn't even think of getting a part-time job, a temporary job. Because I did an intern job at a not-for-profit economic development organization and I thought for sure that this internship would lead me to a career, a job, right after school. So I graduated, and my money was running out. I decided to take a part-time

> job, you know, so I could look for permanent employ-
> ment. Then I ran into my friend Rick and he was doing
> temporary work at the Option, which is the agency I
> worked—I'm now still working—for. And he said, you
> know, "Why don't you go ahead and try it?"

Bob followed his friend's advice and had been working at the agency for
slightly over a year at the time of our interview.

Pamela experienced similar vocational disappointments after graduating from a midwestern state university with an advertising degree. At
first she believed she would be able to find work in a Chicago advertising
agency. She moved to the city with her boyfriend and a small reserve of
money. During her first year she pursued copywriting positions:

> I graduated from college in December of '86 and tried to
> write ads forever and ever. And then ran out of money
> that I had saved and started sponging off from Scott. I
> didn't have any money at all. I was broke. I was eating
> Campbell's soup. Actually, I was watering Campbell's
> soup down so much that it wasn't even soup anymore. So
> that's why I started working temp.

With her money running low and her confidence lagging, Pamela joined
the payroll at a temporary rather than an advertising agency.

Divorced Homemaker Seeks Permanent Position

Displaced homemakers, like other displaced workers, also
frequently take temporary employment as a stop-gap measure (Moore
1963; Leone and Burke 1976). Through various circumstances, such as
divorce or widowhood, many previously non-wage-earning women find
themselves seeking entry into the paid labor force. Many recently divorced women, for example, attempt to use temporary employment as
both a transitional stage and an entry point to the labor market. Though
the temporary industry uses a rhetoric of "skill development" and "work
experience" to attract these displaced workers, the reality may be that
there are few alternatives available (see Landers 1989).

Susan, for example, had partially completed the requirements for a nursing degree in her early twenties. But, like many women in her generation, she had abandoned her schooling before completion of her program when marriage and children intervened. Her husband worked, providing wages and benefits for the family, while she remained at home managing the household and raising their two children. When her marriage ended in divorce, Susan, in her forties, had little work experience in the paid labor force; like many newly divorced women, she found herself facing a precipitous decline in income and standard of living (Weitzman 1985; Newman 1988). "It was rather frightening when all of a sudden, bingo, I'm on my own. What do I do?" Eventually unable to meet the payments on the home in which she had raised her family, she moved into a suburban YMCA until she could get back on her feet. It was there that Susan met a woman who knew about temping.

With the assistance and encouragement of her friend, and with few other opportunities available to her, Susan entered the labor market in her early forties as a temporary secretary:

> What happened was I lived at the Y for a while after my divorce. And a girlfriend of mine that lived there was working down here in the Loop. And she was temping. That's how I got into it. She said, "Why don't you come downtown?" And I said, "I can't go downtown." You know? And she said, "Well, I'll be down there. I'll walk with you and show you how to get places. But temp and then you're not committed to one job. And you don't have to say, 'Well, I don't like it down here.'"

Eventually, Susan parlayed one of her temporary assignments into a permanent secretarial position.

Job Changer Seeks Permanent Position

Temporary employment, at least initially, may seem an acceptable, quick-fix solution to dissatisfied, angry, or burned-out permanent employees. Temporary employment, by offering the prospect of readily available work on short notice, offers independence from bad

jobs as well as from the misfortunes and economic hardships of joblessness; even if a replacement position cannot be found immediately, one
"can always work temporary." Like other joblessness safety nets such as
unemployment insurance, however, the benefits of working as a temporary may be less generous than expected.

Shelley, for example, left an emotionally draining social service career
with plans to enter the private sector but without a replacement position
secured:

> I was working with abused children. I had been working
> at this agency for a number of years and I was burnt out.
> And I thought I can leave this and go temp. I thought
> that would help save my sanity. And I also wanted to get
> into business. I honestly thought that it would be better
> to come into business from temporary work rather than
> from social services. There's a kind of stigma attached to
> the social services in business.

Shelley registered with a temporary agency, which sent her on a handful
of assignments.

On one of her first assignments, at an advertising agency, she was
offered a permanent position—she accepted and "went permanent."
Eventually, Shelley became unhappy in this position:

> I decided to go back to temping and try to find some-
> thing that I did want to do. I thought it would be a short
> period of time, but it was two or three years that I ended
> up doing this temporary work. I'll never quit without
> another position again. If I knew what I know now
> then . . . because, you know, when you're in a permanent
> position you can ask for what you want a little easier, in
> terms of salary and other things.

Shelley's second stint as a temporary was much longer than she anticipated or desired—and much less positive. The availability of temporary

gnments was irregular and insufficient, leaving her with a less
quate income. In order to make ends meet, she occasionally
meals and went without health care and other basic services.

Lifers

The "lifer," a career temporary by choice or personal defi-
ame up quite frequently in my interviews with both temporary
ors and workers, but I found little evidence of its validity as a
nt category.[5] Temporary counselors, for example, attributed lifer
o those with the longest tenure, due sometimes to choice and
nes to deficiency:

> I mean, the initiative in those individuals who come in
> for an interview and they've only worked temporary in
> their backgrounds. I'm a little leery because I think,
> "Why haven't they been able to find a permanent job? Is
> there something about them?" Like you think in your
> head that they can't hold down a permanent job. (Cindy)

> For whatever reason, I would say usually this person just
> has a hard time getting a job or keeping one. And they
> fall into working as a temporary because it's easy for
> them. And there's no real commitment beyond working
> for your service and doing a halfway good job so they'll
> keep sending you out. It just depends on the person. Be-
> cause we have some kind of lower-level clerical people
> who are the sweetest, most darling people in the world.
> And they just want to stay and do this job. This is what
> they want to do. I mean, I guess they're just not inter-
> ested in looking for anything else at this point. (Wendy)

Temporary counselors, embedded in U.S. culture, assume that long tenure in the temporary industry is something that needs an explanation.
Temporary workers, as long as they are considered transitional, enjoy a

reprieve from the stigma attached to long-term or permanent temporaries.[6] If they work as temporaries for too long, however, they risk being thought of as unemployable. As one temporary counselor commented: "Unfortunately, most of the really good, sharp people that come in, if they are looking for a career job or a job, usually they'll find one within two to three months, which is good for them. And good for us too. We make money. They make money. They do a good job of representing us. I mean, nothing is forever." A temporary's transitional status is bounded not only by self-definition but also by expectations of what is an appropriate, allowable, or normative amount of time to work as a temporary. Temporaries who violate these normative assumptions are likely to be involuntarily reassigned to the deviant category of the lifer.

Convinced that I had missed a significant group of temporaries, I began actively seeking lifers to interview. I enlisted the assistance of temporary counselors and temporaries who had specifically mentioned lifers. Though the temporary workers were unable to provide a single referral, the temporary counselors did produce a handful of names. But when I contacted and interviewed these agency-labeled lifers, their stories seemed highly congruent in many respects (except for tenure) with those of other temporaries I had interviewed.

Joanne, for example, had worked as a temporary off and on for thirteen years at the time of our interview. Her first stint as a temporary began in 1978 while she was still attending college. At the age of thirty-six she had worked at several different temporary agencies. And although her work record officially seemed to say "temporary worker," Joanne had accepted and worked in more traditional full-time, permanent positions. In the end, though her agency defined her as a lifelong temporary, she saw herself as an artist and teacher first.

Although not opposed to permanent work per se, Joanne felt that the positions available to her in the labor market were low-skilled, undesirable, and offered little or no chance for advancement.

> If I get to a place and see there's no progression, there's
> no in-house training offered to me, or they don't allow
> me to take it. If it looks like it's really going down the
> tubes, I'll leave first. If there's no place that I can transfer

inside, I'll just go and find another job. And my father has repeatedly told me, "Oh, you're getting too old for this." But I'm a person that I have to be satisfied with what I'm doing. And if I'm not, I'm leaving.

Unable to find unalienating work in the permanent labor market, Joanne sought variety and work satisfaction through the horizontal mobility (Olesen and Katsuranis 1978) provided in temporary employment:

I'm a type person I can't go to one job and be satisfied with doing one thing, year in and year out. I like to do a variety of things, work with a variety of people, and get a chance to circulate. It affords me the opportunity to meet people, to go to different places. And even if I'm downtown with one of my friends or relatives and we're driving in the Loop, I can say, "Oh yeah. I worked at that building. And that building. And that building. And that building."

Temporary employment, while perhaps low-skilled and low-status, offered Joanne a constantly changing work environment.

Similarly, Olivia, a divorced mother and a returning adult college student, had been working in the temporary work force for six years when I met her. It was not, however, her first and only stint of temporary employment. She had first worked in the temporary sector in the early seventies as a relatively recent regional migrant to Chicago. One of her assignments, at a popular radio station, though scheduled to be relatively brief, stretched on to nearly a year. At that point, Olivia went permanent.

After eleven years in this position, Olivia decided to leave. It was more than just fading "glamour," however, that convinced her that it was time to move on. Olivia had been hired as an administrative and clerical worker and there, for the most part, she had stayed. Pushing at the glass ceiling, Olivia decided to quit and seek work satisfaction elsewhere:

I think people have this perception that if you get into a place like that, you're going to stay there until you retire.

> And I don't have that feeling about it. I just felt like after
> being there for that long I was ready for a change. It
> wasn't that I had any other change lined up. I just got
> really tired of the place. And I didn't really see any places
> within the company that I wanted to go to. So I guess, I
> don't know if it's just imagined, but I keep thinking that
> if someone doesn't know me and they find out that I'm
> no longer there, either I got the ax or "What hap-
> pened?!" When essentially I gave them a two-week
> notice and said I was leaving.

Although unwavering in her conviction that leaving her position was the
right thing to do, Olivia was nevertheless aware of the possibly unsym-
pathetic judgments of others. Consequently, she avoided revealing her
work history to temporary clients and supervisors as much as possible.

Counter to the stereotype of the lifer who is unemployable on a
permanent basis, Olivia was frequently offered the chance to go permanent while on assignment with client companies:

> I would say most every assignment that I can think of,
> they've asked if I'd be interested in a permanent position.
> If not actually the job that I'm doing at the time, I would
> be interested in something else within the company. But
> I'm not finding things that are that interesting. And I
> don't think I'm being too picky. I'm certain that I'm
> more selective now. And I would demand more. It's not
> that these companies would be bad to work for, but I
> think that there's something better out there.

Although she refused to accept a position in these client companies as a
secretary on a permanent basis, she paradoxically worked as a "temporary" secretary for six years—often returning to the same companies over
and over:

> KH: But there are a handful of companies that call
> you back?

O: Yeah. And for the most part I'll go back to them, as long as I know that it's not going to be for a real long period of time. Because I'll put up with things as a temp that I would never put up with as a full-time person. Most of the jobs that I get are fine as long as they're temporary. They're not jobs that I would ever want as a permanent person.

For Olivia, horizontal mobility made the work at least tolerable.

As the getting-into-it stories of Joanne and Olivia show, those classified as lifers may be individuals who, though not unemployable, have experienced disappointments with the permanent labor market positions available to them. In other words, it's not that they choose temporary employment because it's wonderful and desirable, but that their permanent work alternatives are confining and unsatisfying. Long tenure may be a way of seeking horizontal variety, and thus tolerability, in an otherwise unrewarding and low-status secondary labor market (Olesen and Katsuranis 1978; McNally 1979).

Sidebets

For a minority of temporary workers, a framework of choice may be at least partially appropriate for explaining their participation in the temporary work force. These "sidebet" temporaries (actors, musicians, artists, students, and the like) support alternative careers, identities, or pursuits through their temporary employment. Although some consider their temporary employment a transitional stint—expecting eventually to be paid in their chosen field—others, never expecting to earn an income from their vocations, reject standard definitions of success linked to remuneration and pursue an alternative career because it is what they want to do.

Actor, Artist, Consultant Seeks Paying Gig

Working as a temporary, then, is often a voluntary accommodation to the necessity of making ends meet. Among actors and other artists, temporary employment (alone or in conjunction with other forms of service sector work) is often used as a routine solution to earning an adequate income while actively pursuing a career in the extremely tight labor market of the arts.

> I'm very happy doing what I'm doing. I love the theater companies that I'm in. I feel they all have a very important mission to fill. I love the messages that we're getting to kids. And so, you know, temping gives me enough money. (Jon)

> I started temping in January of '90. I had just graduated from school with my master's in music performance. And there are very few jobs for a music major. I pretty much thought that this would really work with my schedule, because of auditions. I could get the day off when I wanted. (Bobby Jean)

Acting as a profession, for example, offers a steady and livable income to relatively few of its practitioners. Most paid theatrical engagements are Equity (union) productions. And even if one has been lucky enough to join Equity (a questionable proposition),[7] less than 10 percent of all Equity performers are actively working in show business at any particular time (Witchel 1991; see also Cavett 1990). The actor/waiter combination is a cliché in the theatrical world,[8] but the actor/temp combination is also quite common (see Moore 1963).

Steve, an Equity performer, worked solidly in the theater, supporting himself for three years, yet eventually found himself between shows and without an income. It was during this acting lull that he got into temporary employment as a means of economic survival:

> It was right after college that I moved to Florida and was a gypsy actor for a while. Just went from show to show to show to show. So I started temping about three years after I graduated college because I got back into the city and I had no job. I was on unemployment. I finally said,

okay, my unemployment is going to run out in one
month. What do I do? I temp.

Similarly, Daniel accepted temporary work to support his chosen career as an independent film maker:

> I was working sort of back and forth on this documen-
> tary film project. I said, well, this is what I want to do.
> I'm forty and most of my life I've been fairly unhappy
> with basically what I've been doing as an occupation.
> This is what I want to do, so I'm going for it. You know,
> I shouldn't paint such a bleak, dramatic kind of thing. I
> tend to do that. That's the artist in me. It looks good this
> time. You know you're doing temporary work to make
> ends meet a little bit. But you're basically doing what you
> want to do.

Though film making apparently provided Daniel with many other rewards, it did not give him a steady or livable income. Indeed, all the
performers I interviewed were "working" artists (performing for pay on
an occasional, regular, or semiregular basis), yet none earned a predictable enough living to subsist without other sources of income.

Student on Break Seeks Summer Job

Full-time students on leave for seasonal breaks also join the
temporary employment sector as sidebet temporaries. These comings
and goings are annual events for the temporary industry. Indeed, many
agencies recruit summer help through the placement centers of college
campuses. Company newsletters welcome college students to the organization in the spring and bid them farewell in the fall. Although the
college student, undergraduate or graduate, who works as a temporary
on academic breaks is not simply a myth (it is, after all, also how I got
into it),[9] the industry's image of the "chipper co-ed" trivializes and mis-
represents the economic reasons for which most students seek out this
work.

Kirk, a graduate student in philosophy, for example, turned to temporary employment during semester breaks, when his funding was interrupted, as a primary means of income. He had first worked as a temporary over the summers while pursuing his undergraduate degree. As a graduate student, he found temporary employment the least horrible option of several unattractive employment alternatives: "I guess I could wait tables. But then, you know, I also feel like I'm twenty-eight years old. I'm going to be graduating with a Ph.D. soon. I don't want to be carrying food to be . . . you know. It's very difficult. Summers are very hard." Unable to seek the professional employment he desired because of his liminal status as a graduate student, Kirk instead sought a variety of "menial" seasonal occupations. Few of these seasonally available occupations, however, supported the conception of self that he was actively attempting to construct.

Not only did Kirk find temporary work demeaning; he often found the supply of assignments inadequate. With many unassigned, and therefore unpaid, days, he experienced difficulty in meeting his summer expenses. His girlfriend had, for most of the summer, been supporting them both: "I really can't stand it. She leaves at eight-thirty and gets home at five-thirty or six and she's totally exhausted. She can't stay up past eleven at night. And I feel really guilty 'cause she wouldn't have to be working quite so crazy if I were getting any money in at all. But it's difficult for both of us." Fortunately, Kirk would soon have his Ph.D. and could begin working as an adjunct (read "temporary") professor while searching for a tenure-track (read "real") position.[10]

Conclusion

Stereotypical industry images seriously misrepresent and underrate the economic motivations and limited choices behind most temporary workers' employment. Academic analyses that uncritically echo the temporary industry's rhetoric, failing to examine seriously the role of labor market forces in the growth of the industry, have also contributed to the construction and perpetuation of cultural myths about temporary workers. Consequently, the beliefs that temporaries prefer temporary to full-time work schedules, are secondary wage earners, or possess grave characterological flaws remain ubiquitous. These myths are used to deny, obscure, or justify the lower wages, exclusion from health care plans, and other problems confronting temporary workers. Thus rendered invisible, these problems are presumed not to exist because others (male breadwinners) are already providing for secondary workers. Alternatively, these problems are simply the costs associated with choosing temporary employment or the deserved moral outcomes of personal failings.

The "getting into it" narratives I present suggest another framework for understanding an individual's location in the temporary employment sector. This approach focuses outward, away from the individual, to structural and economic constraints that make securing a good job in today's economy extremely difficult. Though some temporaries were indeed pursuing sidebet careers, most preferred full-time work in the primary sector with permanency, predictable wages, internal advancement, and the provision of employer-sponsored benefits. Such jobs, which many temporary workers felt they were qualified for and entitled to, were difficult if not impossible to obtain.

3 *Getting Work*

KH: Are you working now as a temporary?
G: I'm hoping to. I've been back for about five weeks.
      And the Option only got me four days of work
      the whole month of July.

Temporaries, willing and eager to work, often find themselves with time off instead, time off that can be catastrophic for a worker living at the edge of his or her budget. Although temporary employment increases staffing flexibility for businesses, it does not necessarily increase scheduling flexibility for individual temporary workers. Yet the irregular work schedules of temporary workers, rather than being seen as reflections of the scarcity, cyclical nature, or irregularity of assignments, are interpreted as evidence of individual temporaries' exercising their scheduling "preferences," "freedom," or "flexibility." This myth of temporaries' scheduling flexibility masks the often deficient or sporadic supply of temporary work.

Additionally, though it is assumed that a temporary's unscheduled time is time off, leisure time, or personal time, temporaries often experienced and referred to unscheduled breaks as "down-time." Uncertainty about future assignments, and temporaries' unpaid yet time-consuming efforts to secure work, circumscribed and limited their leisure time and leisure activities (Negrey 1990, 1993). Fearing down-time and uncertain about actual scheduling practices, temporaries often find themselves in dependent, vulnerable, and sometimes manipulative relationships with their temporary agencies and client supervisors. Rather than choosing when to work out of a plentiful supply of options, temporaries have had to develop strategies to ensure access to a steady supply of work.

The Flexibility Myth

While permanent workers are constrained to work the full normative work week, at hours specified by their employers, temporaries are presumed to have more flexible work schedules, to be free from these social controls and restrictions. Fiona McNally (1979), for example, argued that having choices and making decisions about total hours worked and where, were "principal advantages" of temporary over permanent employment (147). Virginia L. Olesen and Frances Katsuranis (1978) similarly maintained that the scheduling flexibility of temporary employment allowed temporaries "a feeling of greater control" over their work: "The fact that they could and did say no to certain assignments gave them a feeling of greater control than many other workers have. Permanent employees who refuse work assignments risk dismissal, censure, or at least their supervisor's displeasure. Temporaries could say no with less risk" (326). Temporaries, hypothetically at least, retain the right to determine both the conditions and hours of their work.

Temporary workers thus are often portrayed as picking and choosing both when and where they want to work (Moore 1963). If the assignment is too far from home, the hours are inconvenient, or the client is known to be unpleasant, the temporary simply refuses to accept the assignment. If the temporary finds the assignment disagreeable or a pressing engagement materializes, he or she simply requests to leave or terminate the assignment. If a doctor's appointment, full-time job interview, additional theater rehearsal, or child-care emergency arises, the temporary simply takes the time off. In this portrayal, temporary workers, presumably freed from the constraints inherent in permanent employer-employee relations, have a great deal of discretion and control over their work schedules.

Temporary workers often believed that temporary employment offered more flexibility. During interviews I heard temporaries say over and over again, like a mantra, how the lack of commitment and greater scheduling flexibility were the "best things" about working temporary:

> KH: Is there something that you think of as the best thing about temping?
> O: The best thing I think is the flexibility. The fact of knowing that I'm not locked into something. And that's pretty much it. Yeah. I can't really think of anything else that stands out. The fact that I can get time off if I need it. And even have the right to turn down an assignment if I want to.

Temporary workers believed that they, like the hypothetical temporary of the industry literature, had the right to exercise their scheduling preferences—accepting or refusing assignments at will, terminating or quitting others, even interrupting or taking time off during an assignment. Many temporaries also believed that they could choose where they wanted to work, avoiding uncomfortable, unpleasant, or unsatisfying assignments:

> You have a commitment but you don't. Meaning if you're on the job, a permanent job, you've already made a verbal commitment to the company. "Yes, I will serve you until the time when . . . " But as far as the temp, you can come and go as you please. If you don't want to go back, fine. If you want to go back, fine. (Joanne)

When I probed for actual instances of temporaries exercising or benefiting from scheduling flexibility, however, I found that such incidents were few and far between. Indeed, all this enthusiasm about the greater flexibility of temporary employment seemed somewhat problematic. Ruby, for example, claimed early in our interview that flexibility was the best part of temping, yet she had taken only three (unpaid) sick days during a seven-month temporary assignment: "Time off you can take. It's sort of hard, though. They say you can look for a job while you're working, but it's sort of hard to when really you're working. You already told us this is a long-time assignment. Somebody's depending on you. I felt guilty. I even felt guilty when I was sick." I routinely asked about the "best part of temping" at the end of each interview, and even temporary workers who had talked at length about scheduling constraints and problems would, with great sincerity, tell me that flexibility was the best part of temping.

Helen, catching herself about to give the standard answer of flexibility, perhaps best summarized the provisional nature of a temporary worker's scheduling rights:

> What is the best thing about it? Well, I would say flexibility, but I haven't taken advantage of that at all. I have not been flexible. I haven't just said, "God. I feel like going to museums today. I don't want to go in." I've never done that because I feel too constrained. I would only use it if I had something absolutely pressing that I had to do.

Actively exercising scheduling flexibility was not a regular or routine event of temporary employment.

The Availability of Work

The option to exercise scheduling flexibility is predicated on the notions of plentiful work and plentiful financial support. Temporary workers, however, frequently had neither. Unlike a permanent or full-time worker, who is ensured a relatively steady supply of work and a predictable income, the temporary worker has a highly variable supply of work and, consequently, income. A permanent worker's income may periodically be adjusted in light of merit reviews and seniority, but any change in the temporary worker's income is based almost exclusively on variations in the total number of hours worked and the type of work. As Kimberly noted: "When I started, somebody mentioned that, 'Oh, the better you are at these programs, the higher-priced jobs you'll get.' And that's true. You get paid higher to be a word processor than you do being a receptionist. But there's no merit." Within skill levels or occupational specialties (such as data entry clerks, receptionists, and word processors) temporary workers earn relatively constant wages. Temporary word processors in Chicago, for example, earned an average of $8.89 an hour in 1987 (U.S. Department of Labor, Bureau of Labor Statistics, 1988, 27).[1]

There are minor wage differences between agencies, but a temporary cannot significantly increase his or her hourly rate with either higher seniority or increased word processing proficiency alone. From the temporaries' perspective, then, "keeping busy" without unpaid days off is one of the few mechanisms of control they have over their income. Nevertheless, many temporaries find themselves on any given day with unassigned and unpaid down-time. Indeed, the industry's ability to keep people busy varies and is highly contingent on general economic trends and conditions (Moore 1963; Olesen and Katsuranis 1978; McNally 1979; Berck 1992). In the fifteen-week period from October 15, 1990, to December 21, 1990, for example, I was scheduled to work only thirty-four of the forty-eight days I requested assignments; nearly one-third of my available work time was down-time. One analyst estimated that only one-fifth of all agency-registered temporaries were on an assignment on any given day (Ten Kate 1989, 34).

Temporary counselors acknowledged the often sporadic and unpredictable supply of temporary assignments. My temporary counselor explained that, although she wanted to place me on assignment, the agency was receiving few orders for temporary help. Another counselor commented: "I'd say, though, two years ago [1989] it was easier for us to keep people busy that wanted to be busy all the time. Because now, even the ones that want to be on long-term assignment and be continuously kept busy, the jobs are not there anymore" (Cindy).[2] The supply of assignments and the supply of temporary workers rarely existed in a one-to-one ratio.

Temporary workers' concerns with obtaining work emerged spontaneously and frequently in my interviews. For example, temporaries tended to evaluate their temporary agencies and counselors on their ability to provide an adequate supply of jobs. Linda said of the temporary agency she was currently registered with: "So far, I like my temporary agency. But they don't give me enough jobs. I don't know why not. I don't know if they don't have enough jobs or if I'm not high enough on the list or what." Phrases such as "She got me work," "They found me work," "She kept me busy," or conversely "They have long lag times," "They don't have enough jobs," or "She doesn't call me much," appeared repeatedly in my interviews. Their prevalence suggests not only the importance of an adequate supply of work to temporaries but the extent to which securing assignments was a routine problem.

Uncertainty and Dependent Vulnerability

Temporary workers rarely have adequate and reliable information about how their agencies actually match available assignments and workers (Olesen and Katsuranis 1978; 9 to 5 1986; Gottfried 1992). In this environment of uncertainty, temporary workers expend a great deal of time and energy searching for explanations about why they are not getting work. During interviews temporaries speculated about perceived personal inadequacies or mistakes, overt racial or gender discrimination, and supply and demand in the labor market:

> A lot of summer assignments go out in June. So if you don't get a long assignment in June, there's a glut of college women on the market. There's always somebody who is willing to supply for a lower wage. They come in at, like, seven or eight bucks over the summer. Why pay someone twelve dollars an hour when they can pay seven? (Aleshia)

Although many of these interpretations seemed plausible, temporary workers were ultimately operating with incomplete information.

This uncertain environment led temporaries to believe that any transgression they committed against their agency would result in punishment, primarily work deprivation. In a labor market in which other employment or work opportunities are scarce, employers can extract a great deal of worker discipline through this mechanism.[3] Barbara Garson, for example, found that managers at McDonald's—another source of "flexible" jobs—manipulated employees into working at the store's convenience, rather than their own, through depriving them of work as a disciplinary action. As one manager explained:

> When you first sign on, you give your availability. Let's say a person's schedule is weeknights, 4 to 10. But after a week the manager schedules him as a closer Friday night. He calls in upset, "Hey, my availability isn't Friday night." The manager says, "Well, the schedule is already done. And you know the rule. If you can't work it's up to you to replace yourself." At that point the person might quit or he might not show up or he might have a fight with the manager.
> So he's fired?
> No. You don't fire. You would only fire for cause like drugs or stealing. But what happens is he signed up for thirty hours a week and suddenly he's only scheduled for four. So either he starts being more available or he quits. (Garson 1988, 32–33)

Workers who are solely dependent on their wages, work nonstandard employer-controlled schedules, and expect to continue getting work learn quickly to meet both the direct requests and the perceived needs of their employer.

Uncertainty and fear of work deprivation placed temporaries in a relatively powerless position vis-à-vis their agency. Dependent on others (their temporary agency and client supervisor) for present and future work assignments, temporaries were vulnerable to these others' whims. In response, temporaries developed strategies based on beliefs about what personal actions and behaviors would please these others and consequently ensure an adequate supply of work. Often these strategies took the form of attempts at ingratiation: efforts to "get in with the agency" and "get in with the client." Alternatively, some temporaries adopted a strategy of "looking out for number one."

Getting In with the Agency

Developing a positive relationship with the agency, primarily through a relationship with temporary counselors, is one frequently used strategy. Temporaries attempted to forge personal ties and minimize the counselor's routine work problems through putting the counselor's "needs" before their own. Temporaries believed they could curry favor and be offered work assignments on a regular basis through sacrificing their flexibility, portraying themselves as dependable and exceptional workers, and making frequent contact with their agencies.

The Sacrifice of Flexibility

Temporaries reported that they rarely turned down, quit, or interrupted an assignment for fear of retribution from their agency counselors. Although temporary workers are advised that they "always have the option to decline an assignment" (Right Temporaries, Inc. 1989b, 2), many suspect or quickly learn that refusing assignments should be done sparingly if at all:

> I sometimes feel a little like there are . . . I don't know if this is true. Maybe you would know from talking to people who place, but is there, like, this good list and bad list? Or is there this list of people who are, like, in the loop and they're going to be placed, like, bang, bang, bang, bang? And then if they can't do it, then you go to this alternate list or something like that? Maybe if you turn them down three jobs in a row or something? Or two jobs in a row? (Kirk)

Fearing retribution in the form of down-time, Kirk and many of the other temporaries curtailed or minimized the use of their "option" to refuse assignments, frequently adjusting other commitments or engagements to accommodate their temporary employment.

Temporaries believed, at least at first, that they would be allowed to refuse to return to a work setting or assignment they found unpleasant. Shelley, for example, asked to perform what she considered "inappropriate" nonclerical tasks on an assignment, requested not to be sent to this particular client company in the future:

> I had finished the work that they had asked me to do. And I went to my supervisor and asked if she had any more work for me to do. And she said, "You can get me some cigarettes." And I refused. I told her that I wasn't there to get her her cigarettes. And then there were a couple of people changing offices and they told me that I could clean their offices. I refused to do that too. I wasn't hired to clean offices or get cigarettes. And I asked my agency never to go back there. But then I felt like the agency would punish you. All of a sudden you'd have a week without any work at all. Every time you'd call in, you'd hear the same thing, "I'm sorry, we don't have anything."

Out of fear of work deprivation, Shelley learned to tolerate more abuse, or to shift her "anger boundaries" (Hochschild 1983), to ensure access to future assignments.

Other temporaries reported similar types of incidents. For example, Helen, a Jewish woman, tolerated offensive jokes from one of her temporary supervisors in order to keep a long-term assignment:

> I've wanted to quit, like, several times. I was working for the director of personnel at a university. And he told racist jokes all the time. Told a lot of black jokes. Said a few things about Jews that were sort of hostile. I didn't want

to be part of that. I didn't want to work there. I just hated it. But again it was a longer assignment and I thought well, that's good because at least it's steady. At the time I'd been getting spotty things. Like two days here, two days there. And you're only working two days a week, which is catastrophic if you're dependent on that check!

Mike, a laid-off banker and a gay man, sat quietly fuming while his temporary supervisor made homophobic remarks and inflammatory comments about people with AIDS. Mike wanted to voice his dissent, but the fear that he would lose his long-term temporary position effectively silenced him.

Regardless of how unpleasant, low-paid, or monotonous, any work is often better than no work at all to a temporary worker at the limits of his or her budget and without access to traditional safety nets such as unemployment benefits. Many temporaries reported persevering in unpleasant assignments out of financial desperation: "I'd say Gothic Life Insurance was pretty brutal. It was stuffing envelopes and working for someone you were . . . Most people were probably eighteen times more competent than the supervisors were. But I was just really desperate to be making any cash at all, so I stuck that out" (Natalie). Such reports contradict images of temporaries who earn nonessential income and freely exercise their scheduling flexibility and preferences.

Despite fears of work deprivation, temporaries did occasionally terminate unpleasant temporary assignments. Temporaries related these stories with a passion frequently absent from the rest of their narratives. Quitting was a rare and notable event. For example, although she recalled several unpleasant assignments, Mary quit only one during her several summers as a temporary secretary:

KH: Have you ever left a job?
M: Yes. I was working for a lawyer here in Chicago last summer. And I was really broke. I needed money desperately so I said, "Yes, I'll take it." The lawyer was

> such a fussy man. He had had a secretary for ten years.
> He was very set in his ways. She knew what he wanted. I
> didn't. He assumed I would know. He had to basically
> retrain me, and I could tell that he resented it. He kept
> saying maybe you could come in the day after tomorrow.
> It was nothing steady. And so I said this is ridiculous. I
> just have to get out of here. I can't stand the man. You
> have to give a little with a temp. You can't expect a temp
> to do what a secretary of ten years has done for you. I
> called the agency and they said, "Yes, we'll get you out of
> it. Just tell them you're coming in. And then we'll call."

Temporaries attempted to minimize the detrimental effects of quitting by determining the conditions under which quitting would be viewed as legitimate or illegitimate by their agencies and framing their leave-takings accordingly. Daniel, for example, learned that both the manner and the timing of termination are quite important:

> I just said, "I'm sorry. I just have to go." Now, see, if I
> hadn't been honest, I could have said, "I have to go
> home because I'm ill." See, that was the slick thing to do,
> but I was just having a nervous breakdown that day. "I've
> got to go!" Oh God. I remember that so well. And that's
> when I said I'll never, as God is my witness, I'll never do
> temp work again.

Daniel, who eventually took back his vow never to do temp work again, felt that this incident put him on his agency's "shit list."

Others believed that the quality or length of the relationship between the agency and the temporary determined whether or not a temporary could terminate an assignment without penalty. Some temporaries, including myself, learned that having a proven or lengthy record of service appeared to provide more leeway in terminating assignments. I requested to terminate prematurely my very first temporary assignment, an extremely unpleasant, low-paying, data entry job in the credit department of a major Chicago department store. After two weeks without a new assignment (or a source of income) I came to believe that I had been black-listed at Active Temporaries and I registered with another temporary agency. When I received an assignment, one that required a commute of an hour and a half (including a train and a bus), I hung onto it for as long as possible.

Still other temporaries requested that their agency pull them from unpleasant (or low-paying) assignments and reassign them elsewhere. Uncertain of the veracity of their counselors' claims that no other assignments were available, however, temporaries were sometimes manipulated into staying. Patsy experienced frustration when she requested reassignment through her temporary agency:

> But a lot of times I go on these indefinite assignments. It just seems like so far no assignment has ever really ended for me. It's just like I get to the point where I can't stand the job or I'm ready to leave. I didn't become a temp to spend six months at one place. So I'll go on vacation or something. And they'll get someone else in there. And when I come back I can get a new assignment. Because the counselor is generally reluctant to pull you off a job and put you on another one. Up until then I would say to my counselor, "I'm really tired of this assignment. I want one that pays better." And she just wouldn't act on it. Leaving town is leaving town.

Patsy, unable to exercise her scheduling flexibility legitimately, resorted to a strategy that imposed a period of down-time. For temporaries without financial cushions, however, this strategy is difficult or unacceptable.

Through fear of down-time or work deprivation, temporaries are limited in their ability to refuse or quit assignments. But are temporaries allowed to exercise greater flexibility within assignments? Can they interrupt an assignment for an hour or an afternoon for an audition or a doctor's or dentist's appointment? Are temporaries allowed greater flexibility in their starting or ending hours? Can a temporary request to work from eight in the morning until four in the afternoon so that he or she can fulfill an obligation at four-thirty? Again, the answer is provisional.

Temporary assignment orders are placed for a worker with specific skills on specific dates during specific work hours. If an individual temporary's availability does not match the assignment, it will be offered to someone else. Thus temporary workers are constrained to work primarily within the normative business week and day, Monday through Friday, nine to five:

> L: And you have to take these jobs. They're always
> eight to five, five days a week, and you can hardly take
> less than a week. Although I've taken some one-day jobs.
> KH: So if you wanted to work three days free-lance,
> you can't just tell the agency you can only work two
> days?
> L: Well, you can say that, but they won't give you a
> week-long job. They'll wait and see if they get one for
> two days. You know, sometimes companies call and their
> receptionist is sick for a day or something happens and
> they need some extra help.

Temporaries are formally allowed their scheduling preferences, but the "choice," take it or leave it, is often an empty one.

Sergei, an actor who occasionally had auditions or callbacks during office hours, initially thought that temporary employment would allow him the flexibility to come and go as he needed. But he soon found that this flexibility was provisional: "I mean, you're tied into situations where you have to work eight hours. And even though you're working temp, they have a business to run. So they may not want to let you off for a couple hours because you have callbacks or something." Thus, exercising flexibility within an assignment was constrained by the client's preferences, needs, and absolute right (within existing labor laws) to determine both the length and the hours of the working day.

Additionally, time off from a temporary assignment is unpaid time. Kimberly spoke of the economic hardship of taking time off from a long-term temporary assignment:

> I broke my thumb a couple of weeks ago and ended up
> spending the morning at various doctors trying to get
> X rays and stuff like that. And that was really frustrating
> for me. I was being paid by the hour and here I am los-
> ing all this money. They don't care if you're missing the
> work, but you don't get paid for it. And if it was a real
> job, I would have gotten compensated for that time.

Though her agency and client supervisor were understanding about a single morning off to take care of health needs, Kimberly recognized that she alone was required to absorb the costs of her time away from work (and the costs of her health care).

When temporaries did have to interrupt a temporary assignment, it often meant forfeiting the remaining days of the assignment and risking down-time (as in Patsy's fictional vacations). Jon was quite anxious about unexpectedly having to take a day off to fulfill his obligation as an alternate actor for one of the theater companies he belonged to:

> The other day I had a big problem. The guy who plays
> the walrus in the show hurt his leg very severely and was
> not going to be able to do the show. I told the director,
> "I don't think I can do it." He got really nasty with me,
> but I was really concerned because the temporary agency
> staff were counting on me to do this job. The director
> called me and he said, "Look, Jon, I cannot find anyone
> else to do the show tomorrow. Is there any way we can
> work this out?" I said, "Well, I can call the agency, but I
> don't want to jeopardize my future with them."

Jon eventually did perform in the show. Although this interruption caused him to forfeit the remaining days of that particular temporary assignment, he received another assignment from his agency:

> I mean, I know the agency was pissed off because, hey, I
> screwed them. But that's why I temp. It's the first time
> that I've ever had to do something like that. It was an

> emergency situation. And ultimately it worked out okay.
> They were fine about it. They got over it in a couple of
> days. And they've got me work all this week.

It appears, then, that flexibility within assignments is also proscribed and provisional. As Kimberly put it, temporary employment is "great for taking off chunks of time. But it's not the flexible 'Oh, I can schedule an interview for two o'clock in the afternoon and since I'm temping I can take the time off.' You can't do that."[4]

The actual scheduling behavior of temporaries, contrasted with their scheduling preferences, reveals the often highly dependent, vulnerable, and manipulative nature of the relationship between employee and agency. Moore, taking into account the irregular and sporadic supply of temporary work assignments, quipped that the recruiting phrase "Work at your convenience" could be more accurately worded, "Work at our convenience, refuse work at your convenience" (Moore 1963, 158–59). In light of the work-deprivation fears of temporaries, however, the phrase would be more accurate if worded, "Work at our convenience, refuse work at your own risk."

Impress and Never Annoy

Besides sacrificing their scheduling flexibility, many temporaries pursue a variety of other proactive strategies to ensure access to a sufficient supply of temporary assignments. Permanent workers, attempting to curry favor with their employers, directly display their commitment and dependability before their superiors in the workplace—arriving early, skipping lunch, staying late, accepting additional work cheerfully, and generally performing the role of hardworking employee.[5] Temporaries, though physically separated from the counselors they are trying to impress, may use similar strategies in the hopes that successful performances will be relayed by the client supervisor to the temporary counselor through either formal reviews or informal contact. Supervision at the agency level, then, is indirect rather than direct. Temporaries who must rely on their agencies for their most precious resource—a steady supply of work—learn to tailor their performances around their sense of what is likely to be communicated back to their agency counselors.

For temporaries, what is likely to be reported to the agency lies at the extreme ends of a continuum. Average or adequate work performance is unremarkable and thus invisible to the agency.[6] No news may be good news for temporary workers, but positive news is even better. Bobby Jean, for example, reported attempting to make herself valuable to the client company. Superior work performance is something that may be reported to the agency counselors:

> I tried to make myself indispensable and show that I was smart enough, that I wasn't some ditzy person. It was just a necessity for me to do temp work at the time, and I knew that you were getting reviewed anyway. So I thought it was important that you should do the best job that you could, and I always tried to make the job as if I was working there permanently. I felt that if I made the agency look good, then they're going to have an assignment for me. And it was true. They keep their good ones busy.

Performing the role of good employee also meant keeping negative reports from reaching the temporary agency. Daniel, for example, occasionally turned down work to avoid potentially negative feedback: "I have learned that I do not take anything out of the Loop. It's too hard to get to. If I can't get there in one train, it's too difficult to get there. And if you get there late, they don't like that. Best not to take the job." Though other aspects of work performance often went unnoticed, punctuality was extremely visible. Even minor tardiness was noteworthy since time was indeed money. Client companies had an economic incentive to contest a temporary's time card, and such protestations occasionally brought tardiness to the agency's attention. Additionally, time cards listing time in, lunch time, and time out were one of the few regular documents the agency received regarding the completion of the assignment; consequently, time cards took on heightened symbolic importance. Temporaries thus believed that special personal diligence was necessary to avoid tardiness.

In addition, being dependable to their agency, and thus employable, sometimes meant that temporaries swallowed their pride. Helen, for example, returned to a client company that had previously telephoned her temporary agency to complain about her personal appearance:

> And you're expected to dress like Christie Brinkley! Oh,
> it's ridiculous. I wear nice clean clothes. I'm clean. My
> body is clean. I have good breath. I mean, I try to look as
> good as I possibly can. When I first started temping, I
> bought a couple of nice conservative secretarial dresses.
> So I get a call from the temp agency at home at seven-
> thirty at night. And it turns out to be, like, the manager
> of the office. And she's, like, "Helen, how's it going?"
> Fine. Fine. And then she goes, "I don't want you to take
> this the wrong way or anything." And I just, like, have
> this thud. My God, what is it? Does someone think I'm
> not wearing underwear? Or is all that cursing under my
> breath audible after all? I was just mortified. Like, what
> is it?! I felt like I was on death row for temps! So she says,
> "Well, it seems that you're not dressing professionally
> enough. Laura gave me a call." And of course I feel
> horrible.

Although embarrassed and humiliated, Helen remained in the assignment, attempting to conform to the client company's dress and appearance expectations. Her efforts to appease the client were apparently still not appreciated, however:

> So the next week on Friday at three P.M. my counselor
> calls up and she says, "Can you come into the agency af-
> ter work today?" So I go there and she says, "It seems
> that you still are not professionally attired." I started to
> cry. I was just so upset. Can't they see that I'm making

the best effort? And I'm a temp! Everybody knows I'm a temp. I had, like, my pearls, my hair back, makeup. I mean, I was just going the distance; I had made a concerted effort to look better and it still wasn't good enough. And I was so upset. Of course, I break down crying. It was horrible. It was just so offensive! And I didn't even want to go back there. Can you imagine how I felt having to go back after having been twice told that?! It was awful. But on the other hand I've met people who've applied to these temp agencies. Same background as I have. And they're not getting jobs. And I'm, like, "Damn. Maybe I shouldn't be so picky and fussy." And just block that out because I need, I need that money really badly.

And when the agency asked that she return to the same company for another three weeks, Helen, against her expressed preferences, acquiesced.

Calling In

Temporaries know that their relationship with their agency, like other relationships, must be nurtured through frequent contact and communication. Turning the cliché "Don't call us, we'll call you" on its head, temporaries placed frequent phone calls to their temporary counselors to both maintain the relationship and secure temporary assignments. Indeed, the telephone was the major form of contact that most temporaries had with their agency after the initial registration visit. The temporary who waits passively for the agency to call, many temporaries believed, loses out when it comes to getting work.

Temporaries called their counselors frequently, sometimes every day, when they were without an assignment. Although these calls were experienced variously as demeaning and possibly annoying, temporaries felt they were a necessary part of securing a steady supply of work:

Most of the time it's up to you to call. At least that's what I've found. You have to call and say, "Look, I'm available.

What do you have for me?" And really bug them. I bug
my agency all the time. They get tired of hearing me.
But that's part of the whoring aspect of it, I think. If I
don't bother them, they're not going to get me work. I've
gotten to the point where I know I bother them, but I
get work. (Jon)

Additionally, temporaries called their agencies when they approached
the end of an assignment. Daniel, for example, routinely called in on
Wednesdays: "Well, if I'm working a job and it's only for a week, I'll call
them by Wednesday to see what's happening for next week. Let her know
that I'm available. But if I'm not going to be available, I call also. It's just
courtesy." Temporaries believed that they were more likely to have an
uninterrupted string of assignments when they gave their agency appropriate lead time.

Occasionally, obtaining steady work through calling in is complicated
when a client company terminates an assignment unexpectedly. Bobby
Jean, for example, was working in a long-term assignment at an insurance company when the job was suddenly terminated:

> The way they got rid of us was just incredible. We got
> out at a quarter to five every day. And I get home and I
> get this call from my temporary counselor: "You don't
> have to go back tomorrow." You mean to tell me they
> couldn't tell me this before I left? When all the managers
> left with me on the same elevator? They knew before I
> left that they didn't want us anymore. Well, I didn't leave
> any personal stuff there except a cup. Because I hated
> this place anyway. I was ready to pack up and leave on a
> moment's notice.

Consequently, Bobby Jean lost several days of work before she was able to
secure another temporary assignment.

Even temporaries who were scheduled in long-term assignments believed that maintaining their relationship with the agency was extremely
important:

KH: How often do you have contact with the agency now?

M: Since the long-term assignment at Midwestern Bank started, my counselor has not contacted me. But I make it a point to contact her biweekly if not more, just to let her know that I'm still here, even though she knows. But I want her to know that I'm still not being offered a full-time position and I'm still looking for one. And I'm going to need another temp assignment when this is over. Maybe she knows this, but I want to make sure.

The temporary counselor has little reason to contact temporaries in long-term assignments unless there is a problem. Yet temporaries believed that remaining in contact with the temporary agency, if somewhat less frequently during long-term jobs, was necessary to ensure a continual supply of assignments in the future.

Besides maintaining contact and a good relationship with the agency, temporaries used other proactive telephone strategies to gain access to assignments. One widely used tactic, the "morning glory routine," involved rising early and calling the agency for last-minute or same-day assignments:

I'd call in at eight o'clock, and then they'd have me on a list saying this person is up and ready to work. So then they'd get a call in. Why call anyone else? Call the people who have already called you. Say, zoom, call right down the list. If their qualifications matched. So sure, I'd call in right at eight o'clock. You get up, run out the door, tie in hand. (Steve)

This routine, however, only occasionally resulted in a same-day assignment. One temporary counselor, for example, reported that her agency received an average of only one same-day order per morning.

Temporary workers using the morning glory routine often experienced imposed limits on their leisure time—a leisure crunch. Sleeping in or other time-off plans may be circumscribed, without pay, by the agency's provisional promises of work:

> I don't mind doing same-day assignments at all, because on the days that I know that I'm available I'll get myself up and ready. And then call in. And if they have something, great. But the thing that I don't like is when they say, "No, we don't have anything." And then they say, "Well, can you hang around for an hour and wait?" And that usually ends up being an hour wasted, because they wind up not calling after all. (Ginny)

For temporaries, then, the process of securing assignments often results in confinement and the further curtailment of their leisure time. Whereas permanent employees may spend time away from work secure in the knowledge that they have a relatively steady source of employment and income, temporaries must balance the necessity of securing the next assignment against other away-from-home activities and commitments.

Long-Term Commitments

Temporaries often believed that temporary employment would allow them to experience working in a wide variety of assignments, providing both work task variety and labor market information on a broad range of companies and industries, but the irregular and unpredictable nature of scheduling interfered. In the interest of maintaining a steady supply of work, as well as maximizing a variety of other factors, temporaries often remain in, accept, and sometimes begin to prefer long-term assignments: "They mainly put me in long-term assignments, which I liked because I liked a steady paycheck. Most of my assignments were several weeks long. I had a couple that were, like, five months" (Bobby Jean). Securing a long-term assignment eliminated or reduced, at least for a time, the routine problem of getting work, allowing the temporary to relax and to predict with some certainty the size and timing of the next paycheck.

Helen, although at first expressing a preference for week-long jobs, quickly learned that long-term assignments solved many routine problems for the temporary:

> A week is nice, because if there are any cool people, you'll find them. You'll talk to them. Yeah, if you see somebody cool, like, reading *The New Republic* at lunch or something, you'll find them. And you sort of know what's going on. And if it's something like WordPerfect and you have a sample letter, right away I can pick it up. And generally you're not expected to get into the nitty gritty and do a lot of filing because it's just a week. And if you knew for sure that you would have another assignment waiting for you the next week, that would be perfect. You'd be popping all over the Loop, and you wouldn't get so bogged down in the routine. But that's not the way it is. Maybe you finish your one-week assignment and then there's nothing for two weeks. So when they say, "This is a three-week assignment," it's, like, "Whew. Well, I guess that's good."

Not only is the anxiety about securing a steady supply of work temporarily suspended, but anxieties that accompany the beginning of each new assignment are reduced after a period of time in a long-term assignment. Will I be able to find the company? Will I be able to handle the work? Will I get along with my supervisor? Will I get along with the other people in the office? Will there be a place where I can eat my lunch? Such questions are answered early in long-term assignments and can recede into the background until the temporary must go to the next new job.

Getting In with the Client

In addition to "getting in with the agency," temporaries may attempt to ensure access to a sufficient supply of work assignments through "getting in with the client." Developing a positive and personal relationship with the client company supervisor is one frequently used strategy. Temporaries therefore attempt to portray themselves to these supervisors as dependable and competent workers. By minimizing the supervisor's work problems, working hard, and forging personal ties, temporaries believed they could curry favor and stretch the current assignment, maximize requests for their services in the future, or even land a full-time permanent position.

Stretching the Assignment

Once in an assignment, temporaries often attempted to impress the client into extending the assignment, providing them with a few more days of work and income. Natalie, for example, worked hard and appealed directly to the client for an extension of the assignment:

> I went to Gothic Life Insurance. That was mind-deadening. That was the worst one. I forgot, I think I might have done that for four weeks. I think it started out being two weeks. And I kind of begged them to let me stay, because I think it was just like the idea of even having two days without a job. If there was a way to stretch the job, to me it was just stretching the money, whether or not it would have been fun to kind of bounce around to different places. I guess I was nervous when I had down-time. I couldn't afford any down-time.

Occasionally, as in Daniel's case, a client company would voluntarily reward a temporary's job performance by finding additional work: "They only asked for a week, but they extended me for a week. They found all kinds of things for me to do, so I could stay another week. They were really nice." Temporary agencies, of course, also benefit financially from this form of assignment stretching, particularly when it is achieved through more, rather than less, effort on the part of the temporary employee.

Indeed, some temporary agencies offered advice to their temporaries about how to extend the assignment. For example, one temporary employee newsletter contained an article entitled, "How to Stretch Assignments!"

> Do a Self-Performance Check. Are you punctual? Do
> you complete your tasks well and in good time? Ask your
> reporting supervisor and co-workers for suggestions on
> how to improve. Ask your counselor for a performance
> report—they will be glad to assist. Do you need further
> training? Did you get along well with others? Take these
> reports seriously and use them as stepping stones to improve yourself.
> Be Helpful. Offer to help others when your job duties
> allow it. If you show that you're willing to do more than
> what you were originally contracted for, they'll ask you
> back. (Right Temporaries, Inc., Fall 1991, 3)

Agency-sanctioned strategies for stretching assignments were directed at managing the impression that temporaries gave (Goffman 1959) their client supervisors. Agencies, in other words, encouraged temporaries to change their behavior—to view themselves as work objects. Workers were advised to perform labor on themselves: to work to change self, control and manage their feelings, and willingly perform more than "a fair day's work."

Occasionally, temporaries were offered "overtime" work. But since a temporary's official work time was almost always less than forty hours (temporaries were required to subtract lunch time from their total hours, turning a nine-to-five, five-day assignment into a thirty-five- rather than a forty-hour week), temporaries rarely qualified for the mandated time-and-a-half pay allotted permanent employees. Overtime for temporaries, however, often provided a few additional hours at the regular hourly rate.[7]

Maximizing Repeat Assignments

Many temporaries reported that they received multiple requests to return to the same company, filling in for various people throughout the year or working on seasonally recurring projects, over the course of their temporary tenure. Jon, for example, first worked in a major Chicago accounting firm on a long-term yet part-time assignment. Although this job eventually ended, he was requested to return for shorter assignments on an occasional basis:

> They needed someone Mondays, Wednesdays, and Fridays. And it was perfect for me. I loved it. It was the upper echelon of . . . it was the Firm Secretaries' group. So, like, the secretary of the entire American firm. Secretary, male, as in treasurer-secretary, not taking dictation. And it worked out really well for me because I really liked the people I was working with, and they loved me. In fact, they request me now every time they call in for a temp. Whenever they need someone within that department, they will call and ask for me first.

These repeat assignments, like long-term assignments, routinize many of the often otherwise awkward procedures of integrating a temporary successfully into the workplace. Additionally, direct requests, to the extent they are honored by the agency, ensure access to work for temporaries who successfully cultivate relationships with their client company supervisors.

In some cases temporaries who had built up a series of relationships with client company supervisors were kept busy by continuously cycling back and forth through a small handful of companies, working one week in one, the next week in another. Susan, for example, developed particularly close relationships with the human resources personnel in both a large law firm and a real estate development corporation:

> I didn't call my agency. What I did, I would call human resources and say, "Do you need me anyplace else here? I'm through at this desk tomorrow. Do you want me someplace else Friday or Monday?" I was dealing mostly through the real estate corporation myself. I wasn't waiting for the agency to call me up and tell me whether I had another job. I had to work. If they weren't calling

> me, I called myself. And I knew people over at the law
> firm. And if I didn't hear from the temp agency, I'd call
> over to the law firm and say, "I'm available Monday. Do
> you need me?" And they'd say, "Yeah, Susan. Come on
> over." I had to work, so I just did everything on my own.

Although Susan secured her temporary assignments herself, they were still formally channeled and paid for through the temporary agency. Through her proactive stance toward scheduling and the relationship she had developed with her client companies, she reduced the work required of her agency counselor and had steady work during her temporary tenure.

Occasionally, relationships with clients extended beyond the boundaries of one specific work organization. Like secretaries who move up in organizations along with their bosses (Kanter 1977), temporaries sometimes followed, albeit still on a temporary basis, their client company supervisors through interorganizational moves. Olivia, for example, reported the unexpected benefits of networking in temporary employment: "I had worked in an insurance company. And this woman that I had worked for liked me. So when she went and worked at another insurance company, she asked if I could come up there to that one too. So it's turned out to be more networking than I expected. You know, making different contacts." In addition, Olivia reported that clients sometimes recommended her specifically to their business associates in other firms and organizations.

Off-the-Record

Other temporaries, in non-agency-sanctioned arrangements, entered into mutual agreements with the client company supervisor. In essence, the client company and the individual temporary worker agreed to cut the temporary agency out of the relationship and work off-the-record. Trent, for example, worked off-the-record for a company he had previously entered as a temporary:

> The office manager grumbled to me one day about having to pay twenty dollars an hour or whatever. And I

said, "Well, you'd only have to pay me half that if I
wasn't with the agency." So she paid me ten bucks an
hour, and I screwed my agency over. She lived in fear
that they would catch her, but that was ridiculous because she was buying their service. You know what I
mean? It wasn't like she was breaking the law or anything. And she was the one paying. I tried to explain that
to her and tell her not to feel guilty. I sure didn't. And I
got lots more money to do it that way.

Although temporary agencies, not surprisingly, actively tried to dis-
courage special arrangements that removed them from the contract and
thus cut into their profits, these off-the-record schemes occurred relatively frequently.

Temporary workers in off-the-record arrangements worried about being found out by their agencies, jeopardizing future assignment possibilities. Kimberly, for example, described her anxieties about one of these
arrangements: "The first week I worked at Huron through the Option.
And then Huron could not afford to pay the Option, so they offered me
the same salary my agency was paying me without the agency. So I said,
'Okay.' But I've gone behind the agency. . . . So I'm careful about that."
Kimberly, who still depended on her agency for assignments (she worked
at Huron part-time), felt that she needed to be guarded about her arrangement. I heard tales of temporary counselors catching temporaries
in off-the-record arrangements by calling the client company's main
switchboard and asking for the temporary by name when they had
suspicions.[8] In general, however, these fears seemed unwarranted. From
the temporary's perspective, such arrangements provided not only (frequently) higher wages but a personal connection and the possibility of an
ongoing, if irregular, supply of work.

Going Permanent

Besides working off-the-record in informal temporary arrangements, temporaries could reduce their scheduling uncertainty and
their dependency on their agency by "going permanent," or accepting a

full-time job with a client company.[9] Occasionally, a temporary was able to parlay a clerical temporary position into a permanent nonclerical position.[10] Most permanent work opportunities available to temporaries, however, were clerical or secretarial. Some temporaries desired such arrangements and were quite happy to accept them, but others found full-time clerical work problematic or undesirable. Some temporary workers, eventually swayed by the security of a predictable income or the prospect of health benefits, reluctantly accepted this type of position.

On rare occasions a worker began as a clerical temporary and then was able to secure a permanent nonclerical position. Pamela, for example, described how she was "discovered" training full-time secretaries to use new personal computers and software on one of her temporary assignments:

> And pretty soon everybody . . . like, the head of sales administration was, like, "Who is that person?" "The temp. The temporary." And I told him that I was interviewing and blah, blah, blah. So he took my résumé. And he said that they were starting a new department with computer systems. A really weird career path, 'cause now I'm "Senior Business Analyst," which means nothing except that I work with computers. But that's how I got started was Manpower taught me how to use all these word processing programs. I started training secretaries. Somebody noticed. And they offered me, like, a real job.

Although her new position was not in advertising, her preferred career after college graduation, it was a full-time, permanent position paying a comfortable salary—a position she was very pleased to accept.

Similarly, Susan was happy to parlay one of her temporary assignments into a full-time secretarial job. A displaced homemaker, she had entered the temporary employment sector with the hopes of eventually landing a secretarial position. Shortly before she passed the two-year anniversary of her temporary status, she was offered a full-time position with a client company for whom she had worked. She decided that it was

time to "go permanent" both for the security of the regular paycheck and
for the health insurance: "I was starting to get a little nervous, you know?
And I thought, 'Well, it's about time I went permanent.' And it was really
a big decision. A very big decision. But the longer I went, I thought, what
if my appendix bursts? The hospital bill alone would kill me." Unlike
many of the other women I interviewed—particularly those with college
degrees in younger cohorts—Susan did not express the same kinds of
underemployment anxieties about being a full-time secretary:

> I like my bills paid. You know what I mean? My rent. I
> mean, I started out after my divorce living at the YMCA
> with nothing but my clothes. And right now I have a
> three-bedroom apartment that's completely furnished.
> And I don't want one thing taken away from me. I've
> worked too hard for the past five years to get what I've
> got. I'm not losing a thing. And I will do anything to
> save that and myself. You do what you gotta do to sur-
> vive. It may not be what you want to do, but if it brings
> home an honest paycheck, that's what matters.

When I met Susan (she was my client company supervisor on an assignment), she had worked her way up in the company and was a well-
respected executive secretary.

Other temporaries, however, when offered positions that were similar
to the temporary work they were already doing, felt that accepting would
be to settle for underemployment in dead-end jobs that would waste
their hard-won skills or college degrees. Yet these temporary workers
were also ambivalent; the security of permanent work had its appeal:

> I've been offered probably about twelve jobs in the time
> that I've been working temporary. But they were like,
> "Gee. You probably wouldn't want this. You're probably
> overqualified for this." It's, like, "Yes. Everyone is over-
> qualified for this kind of work." It's a very bleak pros-
> pect. I would never, never take any of those jobs. Even
> though some of them pay, I guess, twenty-five thousand

dollars a year for an executive secretary or something. And with times being the way they are, you know, even my parents were like, "Hmm. What about just for a year?" And I was, like, "Never. Never. I'd rather die." (Helen)

The only reason I would take a permanent position with them is for benefits. For a good salary, I would work just about anywhere. But I would be much more accommodating or tolerant of a position if financially it was rewarding. But otherwise I don't think so. Just because you see that they're not going to take advantage of you. You start to feel this brain rot. (Aleshia)

Although the distance from the secretary's cubicle to the manager's corner office is generally only a few feet, it is frequently infinite in social or organizational terms. Recognizing that the corporate ladder does not traverse this carpeted moat, that secretarial work is frequently a dead end, many temporaries, at least at first, politely declined the full-time secretarial positions they were offered. Temporary work for a "little while longer," although not ideal, was a more attractive alternative than either unemployment or underemployment in the secondary labor market on a permanent basis.

Lillian, for example, found herself negotiating the tensions of continuing in temporary work or unhappily accepting a secretarial position. An Asian studies graduate of a small private liberal arts college in the Midwest, she had traveled briefly after graduation and then returned to the United States expecting to enter the permanent labor force. She sought positions through a variety of avenues—employment agencies, want ads, blind telephone calls, and letters. Although she received invitations to interview, most prospective employers seemed more interested in her typing speed than her college degree:

I looked kind of hard. And a lot of what I saw was just secretarial work, which I'm doing now through the temporary agency, which I really can't stand doing. I have a

degree. I should be able to do something a little bit more
substantial. Because secretarial work is . . . I mean, it's an
important function in any company, but it's not something that I want to do any longer. So I'm still doing
temp work.

Lillian, like many of the other temporaries I interviewed, was offered
(without inquiring) permanent secretarial positions while on assignment. She had turned down these offers and continued to look for
permanent work commensurate with her training. But, like many of the
others, as the length of her time in temporary work grew, she began to
doubt her decisions:

The desk that I was working at for two months was on a
paralegal floor, and they asked me, they were looking for
secretaries, "Do you want to stay?" I would have been
their secretary. They would have hired me straight in.
And I was, like, "Well, no, not really." Secretarial work is
something I don't want to do. I don't know why I'm still
doing it. I guess I'm just . . . well, to pay the bills. But I
think I should have a permanent job by now.

Discouraged with temporary employment and with her prospects of
finding a primary labor market position at the time of our interview,
Lillian was beginning to consider taking a permanent secretarial position
at the law firm where she was on a long-term temporary assignment:

I'm really debating it now. I really have a hard time making that commitment. It's just such a letdown. You
think, well, I've been out of school now for a year, and
what really have I done? Not a lot. In the area of work, I
mean. It's just like . . . it would be a letdown. I don't expect to get this job that's paying terrifically, but I would
like something that would build on my skills, so that I
could work closer to my goals. But it's not happening. I

guess when I get really, really discouraged, I will take a secretarial job.

Many of these temporaries eventually found and took permanent positions, positions that they originally considered unacceptable:

> I actually got on the company's permanent payroll, like, the end of April. So I was there a good three months as a temp. At that point, I was kind of looking for a job, mainly because I was working full-time as it was. I wasn't really taking any time off. And every time I took time off, I wasn't getting paid for it. And I didn't have any benefits. None. And I was kind of afraid of, if something ever happens without either my husband or I having insurance, we'd really be up the creek. It really wasn't any different than what I'm doing. (Bobby Jean)

This career path suggests that temporary employment may act as a cooling-out place for workers, particularly women, with "overly" high occupational aspirations. Additionally, there is some evidence that the women were typecast as clerical workers and ended up accepting secondary labor market positions, whereas the men moved directly into positions in the primary labor market.

Looking Out for Number One

Temporaries who attempt to exert control over their supply of work exclusively through the strategies of building ties with their agency counselors and individual client supervisors are nevertheless still quite dependent and vulnerable. There are, however, several strategies that mitigate this dependency and vulnerability. For example, temporaries may increase their supply of work through "temp lies," or deceiving their agency about their abilities; through minute pinching, or time-card doctoring; through registering with more than one temporary agency; or through securing an alternative supply of work and exiting.

Temp Lies

Some temporaries said that they declined assignments rather than risk getting a bad report, but others reported that they played the odds and told "temp lies" in order to get an assignment. Betting that they could learn an unknown software quickly, or at least quickly enough to fake it and get through the assignment, temporaries made dubious claims to their counselors about software competencies and other skills:

> Whenever they called me last summer, "Can you do this?" I would just sort of say, "Oh yeah, I can do that" even if I hadn't done it, which I never would have done first time around temping. Then you run around calling your friends, panicked, "Have you ever done this before?" "What's the keyboard command for this?" (Natalie)

> I learned all of the software on the job. I'd learn a little. I'd read the thing. I'd try to do the tutorial. You know? 'Cause you get more jobs that way. And it is not that difficult, but you do have to know something. So you know, they'd ask me, "Can you do WordPerfect?" And I'd say, "Yeah, I can do WordPerfect." So they'd send me on a WordPerfect job and during that job I'd really learn WordPerfect. They're always saying, "Now these people really want you to have WordPerfect 5.0." And I'd say, "Okay, no problem. Sure, I know that." Right. (Linda)

Given the choice of fibbing and getting work or being honest and having down-time, temporaries frequently chose the former route. Those pursuing this strategy of lying and learning, however, still had to complete their formal work tasks successfully or risk losing the current assignment and possibly future ones. Temporaries often recruited "trainers" or "assistants" from among the permanent staff; consulted friends, manuals, or on-line help systems; or found previously created and formatted document files to use as electronic templates.

Minute Pinching

Some temporaries reported that they extended their assignments, and thus their pay, through the strategy of minute pinching. Through reporting shorter lunches than the ones actually taken, adding half an hour here, fifteen minutes there to their time cards, temporaries attempted to get the most pay possible for "a day's work." Kimberly, for example, admitted "doctoring" her time card:

> I've never been paid for lunch anywhere. Another naughty thing was I'd write down a half-an-hour lunch when I really took forty-five minutes or an hour. It was kind of a new realization when I learned that the Option gets paid much more than they pay me. Figuring, "Fine! It doesn't matter. They can just pay me some more." And it depends on who you're working with and what their schedule is. At the bank, they're hardly ever there. They don't know if I left at twelve-thirty or if I left at one.

Padding the assignment through doctoring the time card is a risky tactic, however. Client company supervisors must verify and sign a temporary's time card before the temporary can submit it to the agency. Occasionally, supervisors challenged a time card, essentially accusing the temporary of time theft, creating embarrassment and the possibility of formal censure from the temporary's agency.

Other "renegade" temporaries used deliberate work slowdowns to extend the assignment. When hired to complete a specific and known project (such as envelope stuffing, photocopying, or form-letter production), the temporary could stretch the assignment by not working at his or her full pace. Kara, for example, was taught by another temporary how to extend assignments through a purposeful slowdown:

> One assignment I did was a mailing for an insurance company. It lasted as long, however long it took me to do this mailing for thousands of people. And here I am being really efficient. I'm doing these as fast as I can. And

this girl came up to me in the office and she said, "If I were you, I'd slow down." She said, "If you want this job to last a little longer, just slow down a little bit. Let it go out." So that's the kind of stuff I would do.

Kirk also reported that he consciously worked slowly on some assignments in order to extend his supply of paid time:

I think temporaries, in general, maybe not in general but a lot of them, extend their work to get as many hours as possible. I mean, it's a classic case of people who are only paid by an hourly wage and not at all in relation to their product. Right? There's no way to imagine that what you're doing is going to have any financial consequences for you based on when you get it done, unless they're going to fire you. But if you go for a temporary job, you're pretty well educated, you're pretty well put together, you know, you're socially skilled, they're going to like you. They're not gonna wonder, "Gosh. It's really taking this guy a long time to get things done." So it just seems like all the incentives are for temporaries to take as long as possible.

A work slow-down had to be carefully managed, however, because a temporary employee who worked too slowly could easily be fired and replaced. Temporaries using this mechanism had to look busy, as if they were working at their full pace, while rationing the flow of work.

Double Registering

Many temporaries reported that they registered with more than one agency as a strategy for ensuring an adequate supply of assignments (see Moore 1963, 10). Ginny, for example, said that she was currently registered with two agencies:

My file has been activated here at the Busy Temps office as well. I haven't gotten an assignment from them in

Chicago. I'm probably going to register with one or two other places, because I need to support myself. And if places are just not getting me assignments, I know so many people who are, like, "Yeah, you have to register with a whole bunch," in order to work consistently enough to earn decent money.

Registering with multiple agencies, however, requires extensive management work on the part of the temporary. Ties with each agency have to be maintained, and the possibility of getting black-listed increases, as temporaries have to refuse assignments from one agency to work for another. Many temporaries believed that it was necessary to conceal the fact that they were working for other agencies from their temporary counselors (see Moore 1963). Consequently, most temporaries reported that they eventually settled into working for one or at most two agencies.

Other Agencies

Even when temporaries were registered and worked exclusively with a single agency, knowledge of the existence of other agencies released them, at least psychologically, from some of the dependency on their agency.

There's so much competition for temp agencies in Chicago that it doesn't mean anything that I work for Busy Temps. With the recommendations . . . I mean, they have to give me a recommendation if I ask for one. I get those work review cards back; they're superior every time. People call back for me. It would be really easy to get another temp assignment. If I want to blow something off, I could. And I could do it quite often. But I enjoy work. I like to keep busy. (Aleshia)

Moving to another agency, however, has its costs. Besides the half-day or more spent registering, temporaries sacrifice the advantages of the longer association with their previous agency. The relationships temporaries have built with their counselors and client companies, relationships that may provide them with a more steady source of work and income, are severed.

Conclusion

The belief that temporary workers by virtue of their employment relations are free from the social controls and constraints built into permanent work contracts is unfounded. Temporaries, in practice, do not appear to have significantly greater scheduling flexibility than more permanently employed white-collar workers. Indeed, temporaries who are willing and eager to work frequently find themselves with time off, or down-time, instead.

Uncertainty and incomplete knowledge about actual scheduling practices, and the routine problem of securing work and thus income, keep temporary workers in dependent and vulnerable relationships with their agencies and their client companies. While client companies enjoy staffing flexibility, terminating the assignment at will (for example, when the allotted work has been completed), individual workers are often at the mercy of both their agencies and their client assignment supervisors. Temporaries attempted to secure an adequate supply of assignments by ingratiating themselves to their agencies and the client companies to which they were sent.

In essence, many temporary workers, confronting their employment and income uncertainties, voluntarily "disciplined themselves" to be compliant, persistent, and productive workers (see Gottfried 1992) in the hopes of securing future work assignments. Ironically, this worker-imposed self-discipline largely benefits the temporary agency and the client company rather than the worker, particularly since the loyalty of temporary workers is rarely rewarded with higher wages, real stability, or better working conditions.

4 *Doing the Work*

We're sure that you, our temporaries, know that we are
deeply concerned with your welfare, the maintenance or
improvement of your lifestyle, and your advancement in
the world of business—through training and exposure to
variable commercial situations which are sure to widen
the scope of your experience and assure your future security. (Right Temporaries, Inc., *The Right Approach,*
Fall 1989)

They send me on all kinds of interesting assignments
where I can increase my skills and improve my knowledge of the business world. (Brochure for Norell)

Temporaries expressed a high level of dissatisfaction with
their work, describing it variously as "boring," "monotonous," "repetitive," "routine," "tedious," "mundane," "menial," "awful," "horrible,"
"terrible," and "lonely." Yet temporary workers differentiated between
better and worse jobs. Linda, for example, indicated an implicit and
informal hierarchy of desirability (Chinoy 1955) when she stated, "This

month I have had very few nasty jobs." Similarly, during one of my data entry assignments, Francine, another temporary, commented, "Busy Temps actually has some good jobs, but sometimes you gotta take some of these to get to those." Through recognizing bad and not so bad, good and not so good jobs, clerical temporaries acknowledged a degree of variability across, but not necessarily within, their work assignments.

Generally, these preferences paralleled the two tiers of full-time clerical work. Routine, single-task, highly rationalized clerical assignments (such as data entry, filing, photocopying, envelope stuffing), which were frequently handled by secretarial pools, were rated as the least desirable assignments and were described as "bad jobs" by temporary workers. Fill-in, replacement, or "coverage" assignments (executive secretary, departmental secretary, and the like), on the other hand, generally staffed by temporary workers only when a full-time employee was absent or unavailable,[1] were rated more highly and sometimes even described as "good jobs."

Hierarchy of Desirability

Because temporaries experience work in a variety of organizations, and because clerical work and job titles are organized somewhat differently from organization to organization, it is often difficult to tell a priori whether any particular job will be good or bad. A temporary accepting a "word processing" assignment in one company might find it to be secretarial in nature (working for a single boss while answering phones, typing correspondence, and completing other light office tasks). In another company, however, the temporary might find a "word processing" assignment to be more clerical or production oriented (working under a general supervisor in a typing pool performing steady and continuous document production). More than the official job title, then, the organization of the work within a particular client company determined the nature of the job.

In describing their experiences, temporaries articulated characteristics or dimensions of the work that defined a "good" or a "bad" job. Kimberly and Helen, for example, elucidated several dimensions in their descriptions of bad jobs:

> Minimal work. Boredom. And not challenging work. I'd much rather be fighting with a spreadsheet, trying to figure out how to set up a spreadsheet, rather than just entering in the numbers. A boss who treats you like a temp and is very much, like, always checking up on you or else totally ignoring you. Doesn't really remember your name. Says, "Oh, I'll just put this here. We'll wait till so-and-so gets back to work with it." (Kimberly)

> The isolation. The lack of benefits. The monotony. The underemployment. Your resources, your skills, your intelligence are not integrated. I mean, there's no change. So I guess just the hopelessness, just the stagnation. The fact that there's never any increase in cerebral activity. Even when they find out more about you, they still don't trust you to take on more. But the loneliness. It's really lonely. Eating lunch by yourself every single day. And no one ever asking you a personal question. Like the secretaries never, ever ask, "Where are you from?" or "What have you been up to?" (Helen)

In general, the dimensions temporaries most frequently emphasized in evaluating their assignments were the degree of autonomy over the work process, the relative degree of mental engagement, and the extent to which opportunities were available for sociability on the job.

Routine Work

At the bottom of the hierarchy of desirability were the routine work assignments. These repetitive clerical tasks, such as steady and continuous data entry, filing, photocopying, and envelope stuffing, were not only the least desirable work in the temporary world but also the lowest paying. Charles, for example, described his worst temporary assignments:

> Stuffing envelopes, filing, copying. Those secretarial jobs. I didn't like that much. Because they were so monotonous very quickly. And you didn't have to engage your brain at all. The ones where you had the least responsibility. The ones that were the easiest, that anybody could do them. Those were the ones that I didn't like.

These jobs, frequently handled in the secretarial pool, were the ones to which temporaries were most likely to be assigned. Management often presumes that this work, pared down to the most menial, manageable tasks, can be successfully tackled by any worker with a minimal orientation and the most cursory period of training. Thus, temporary workers are perceived as ideal low-cost workers for these positions. And, indeed, the majority of temporary workers are hired exclusively for routine, single-task, clerical and administrative support assignments.

Temporary workers are sometimes brought in specifically for jobs that are so routine, tedious, or dangerous that companies are reluctant to ask their full-time workers to take them on (see Parker 1994). Debbie, the supervisor of an in-house data entry division predominantly staffed by temporary workers, acknowledged that much of the work was tedious: "I'll take temps any day. They don't grumble like full-time people do. 'Oh, we have to do this?' They just do it. You know they don't care. They know they're there for tedious work, or relatively tedious work anyway. Some of the stuff would put me to sleep." Other client companies acknowledged using temps for admittedly dull and routine tasks such as opening mail and processing checks. Irene Cohen, president of a New York City temporary agency, stated, "We know certain jobs are monotonous. So we ask people we send there to tell us as soon as they're unhappy, and we'll gladly find them something else" (Kirkpatrick 1988, 112). That is, of course, if "something else" is available.

Besides relatively routine and expected "dirty work," the clerical temporaries I interviewed described a variety of "shit work" assignments that were both physically taxing and dirty. Kirk, although working through a clerical temporary agency, recalled an onerous three-day manual assignment:

> Undoubtedly the worst temporary job I ever had. These two tractor trailers filled with children's toys had been parked at this warehouse and right behind it was a river. It rained incredibly and these trailers flooded. Me and this one other guy had to unload these two huge tractor trailers that were filled with mildewing, festering, wet children's toys. And the two days that we worked were, like, ninety degrees. And these big things just became like tin ovens.

Other temporaries hired for clerical or secretarial work were, on arrival in white-collar attire, asked to distribute fliers on windy Chicago street corners, stock supply rooms, and clean offices and bathrooms. Temporary workers insulate core workers not only from the vicissitudes of the economy but also from tedium, hard physical labor, and disgust.

Coverage Work

At the top of the hierarchy of desirability was coverage work. In these more desirable secretarial, word processing, and receptionist assignments the temporary was often filling in for or replacing a full-time employee or covering an otherwise vacant position. These secretarial positions had resisted fragmentation and dispersion to the pools and remained at least somewhat varied and integrated: "I worked as a receptionist at Rose University for a month. And that was a great job. Because that was like being back with students and stuff. And I was twenty-three. I was booking conference rooms and making sure all the sororities got to use the gym on Tuesdays. Stuff like that. I worked with really nice people" (Pamela). Many of these positions, particularly in their permanent incarnations, offered some autonomy over both the pacing and execution of tasks, a varied range of duties, and ample opportunities for social interaction with others during the course of the work.

Even within these assignments, however, issues of trust, the need for specific organizational knowledge, and attitudes about temporaries' qualifications put constraints on the types of tasks assigned. Many client companies, rather than tackle the difficulties of explaining or supervising the more complex tasks of a position, assigned temporaries only the most pressing duties (such as answering the phone) and asked them to set the rest aside. Even when filling in for an otherwise varied position, then, temporaries are often asked to complete only the more menial or routine parts of the job.

Autonomy

Workers in many occupations express desires for autonomy in their work, but workers with too much autonomy, from management's perspective, cannot be trusted to apply themselves diligently to the work at hand. Control over the work process becomes a central issue of contention between workers and management. Management often believes that the "efficient" use of labor power is the only way to guarantee profitability. "Managers consider the work process and the worker the means—and sometimes the obstacles—to the realization of this goal"; to ensure efficiency, management attempts to control both (Glenn and Feldberg 1982, 209–10).

Temporaries considered good jobs to be those that allowed them autonomy over both the way the work was completed and the way in which they worked. In reaching for a way to describe these aspects of good jobs, temporaries often resorted to telling how their temporary work fell short of previous work experiences. Helen contrasted her current temporary work with her experience in the Peace Corps: "That's why the Peace Corps was so wonderful. It was so creative. You were totally in charge. You almost had too much say over what you did. But it was so challenging. And exciting. And beautiful. And different. And then you come back to the U.S. and you're temping." Similarly, Lillian compared her temporary work to a previous position (ironically) in the career development center at a midwestern liberal arts college:

It's like I'm used to being challenged, taking classes, working on my job. The nontemporary jobs that I've had have been interesting. You meet different people. Like the career adviser thing. There were six of us and the director. And you were pretty much left on your own. You met with the students. If you had a program you wanted to start, you set it up, implemented it. You had a lot of leeway. And in this temporary job I'm doing nothing.

Autonomy allows workers to take initiative, display creativity, accept responsibility, and generally invest themselves in their work. Consequently, workers with greater autonomy can take pride in difficult but well-made judgment calls, creative or elegant solutions to problems, and even in a successfully completed product or job.

Routine Work and Control

The disparity between the desire for autonomy and the lack of autonomy present in temporary assignments, particularly in the most routinized tasks, is dramatic. The subdivision and fragmentation of work, centralizing knowledge and control in the hands of management, "prevents workers from gaining an overview of the total work process, thus necessitating external coordination, supplied by managers" (Braverman 1974; Glenn and Feldberg 1982, 210 [quotation]). Temporaries, who are less likely than other workers to have an adequate conception of the overall work process because of their organizational marginality and short tenure, are often subjected to even higher levels of external coordination. Appearing for work in an unknown company, perhaps without even an awareness of the main product or business, temporaries must await instructions from their client company contacts. The work process for temporaries on routine assignments, then, including the actual division of labor, the ordering and execution of tasks, and the pacing of work effort, is controlled directly by management.

Preventing workers from gaining an overview of the work process also gives management, not insignificantly, the power to control workers. The labor of workers is cheapened and their bargaining position vis-à-vis management is weakened when the work process is simplified, routinized, and fragmented (Braverman 1974). Debbie, a client company supervisor, in a particularly telling discussion, described a struggle over pay rates with temporaries on a long-term assignment within her company, a struggle that was intricately interwoven with issues of knowledge, power, and control:[2]

> We try to defer to the temporary agency as much as possible on pay rates. But I mean, I've had people freak out. "I'm going to quit tomorrow if you don't pay more." Which is fine. I'd love to have them quit. But then my subordinate production supervisors come to me and say, "I can't have them quit. They know too much. They're too valuable." And that's the situation you get in. And if they're good, temps have a lot of leverage. I love it. I'm firing, like, five of them as soon as this one project is done. They're going to take what I call a leave of absence from the company. They're really great temporaries, but they're just too cocky. They know too much. So I'm going to get them out of the circle until they don't know enough, then come back in. I mean, they know too much about the case, the documents. Where they can say, "Oh, how're you going to get on without me?" Well, we'll deal. They're not coming back. I mean, I can't have a temporary try to rule my pay rate. That's ridiculous.

Knowledge is indeed power. Rather than desiring skilled and knowledgeable workers, management in this instance preferred deskilled, unknowledgeable, and consequently powerless workers. The latter are easier to control and exploit. The subdivision of the work process may not always increase the efficiency or the speed with which the work is completed, but it does cheapen one of its components—labor costs (Braverman 1974; Ferguson 1984).

Management control of the work process through personal supervision in temporary work was occasionally extreme. Olivia described a word processing assignment in which the supervisor, as if directly out of a Taylorist training manual, had pushed time management through direct supervision to its limits:

> The supervisor there was like a drill sergeant. She had everything worked down to a routine. I was not supposed to watch a letter being printed. I was supposed to be going on to the next one. It was like factory work. It was an office version of a factory job. I don't know how else to describe it. Because every move had to be precise with no wasted movements.

Temporaries, who because of their temporary status do not have a personal history with the supervisor, may have even less autonomy than full-time employees in the same position. Full-time clerical workers sometimes gain more autonomy in the work with seniority.

Temporaries may be subject to even more intense external supervision than other workers since diligence on the part of management is only relaxed, if ever, when a modicum of trust, built up over time, develops between an employee and his or her employer. Bobby Jean described working in a highly regimented client company:

> The company was terrible to begin with anyway. They were just nasty to their employees. No respect for them, distrust everywhere. They had a lady standing there. If you were two seconds late, you were out the door. They had several temps in this department because they didn't want to hire anyone full-time anyway. And I saw about four of them come and go, because they got rid of them, not because they left.

Rules regulating time (starting time, ending time, lunch time, break time) and personal behavior (appearance, conversing, eating, drinking) are stringently enforced to ensure that temporaries put in a (management-defined) "fair day's work."

Mistrust was sometimes quite serious in temporary work. I was the prime suspect, for example, when a set of tickets to a Chicago Bears game came up missing on one of my assignments. I related the story to Patsy that day after work during our interview:

> KH: Grace came out with four sets of season tickets to the Bears. They were on a perforated thing. She wanted me to separate them. So I separated them out and put them back on her desk. And then she wrote a memo on a legal pad and left it on Julie's desk with tickets to the game this Sunday. And then the tickets came up missing. So for most of the afternoon there was this silent accusation, like, "You know, you're going to get arrested when you try to use those tickets." Dreadful. I, of course, was trying to help find them. I don't even care about the Bears. I was given this really icy shoulder, like, "The temp stole them."
>
> P: Yeah. Kill the temp! Kill the temp!
>
> KH: And then Julie found them. She had tucked them in a folder and then filed the folder away by accident. No one ever flat-out accused me. And no one ever flat-out apologized for suspecting me. But it went from icy cold to everyone being happy smily.

Management's control over the work process can also be more subtle; control can be embodied within the technology. In the organization of data entry work, for example, programmers, along with management, have anticipated and removed nearly all necessary decisions or judgment calls from the actual work. An AT&T systems analyst succinctly stated the rationale behind such planning: "The work must be carefully organized in the programming department so that the great bulk of it can be done by $3.00 an hour clerks with virtually no training" (Paul Smythe, quoted in Garson 1988, 166). Data entry, one of the least desirable temporary jobs, is the epitome of routinized and machine-regulated office work. Charles described working on a data entry assignment:

> It was digital equipment stuff with set screens, set templates where you just punch . . . you go six screens in a row. The first screen has all the set information. You just fill in the blanks and then you hit a key and you go to the next screen and you do that. For each document, you might go through six screens and then you do the next document for six screens. If you didn't glean the right information from the document, that's how you could screw it up.

The content, placement, and format of data to be entered were all predetermined by management and the programming department. Indeed, the only challenge left was in visually "gleaning" the right piece of information. Where the risk of error is minimized, so too is the possibility for taking pride in avoiding it.

Additionally, the more standardized and routinized the work, the easier it is for management to regulate and monitor the level of any particular worker's efforts (Glenn and Feldberg 1982, 210). New systems of work, in other words, have created new systems of surveillance. As Kathy Ferguson notes, clerical workers "are embedded in a system that so automatizes, disindividualizes, and objectifies their activities and relationships that the power relations therein are synonymous with the activities themselves" (Ferguson 1984, 88). By simply observing workers' movements, management can often tell whether or not workers are doing their jobs (Braverman 1974; Glenn and Feldberg 1982, 210). If the work has been reduced to pure typing, for example, any interruption in the steady action of fingers hitting keyboard keys is evidence that the worker is not doing his or her job: "It was horrifying. There was this woman that was like a prison camp guard. If she didn't hear, like, the little click of the keyboard keys, she'd just come bustling in. 'Oh! What's the matter?! Are you confused about something? Is there something you don't understand? Why did you stop typing?' " (Patsy). In essence, interruption in work effort, including any pause in activity or movement away from one's work station, was defined as not working, or time theft. Furthermore, management may now easily electronically monitor a clerical worker by checking the amount of data entered, pages typed, or phone calls logged (Glenn and Feldberg 1982; Cockburn 1985; Garson 1988).

Management may additionally control the worker through enforcing work quotas or determining and setting the pace of the work. Bobby Jean described these production pressures in one of her routine temporary assignments: "You were constantly under pressure to get so many insurance policies out. You had a new shipment every day that had to be put together. Files had to be copied. And there were certain ways of doing things that you had to do it this way." Similarly, in one of my data entry assignments the supervisor set hourly production goals for the temporary staff:

> The supervisor comes over first thing in the morning to give us a pep talk. "Your production is fine. You're getting a good number out, but they're telling me that you need to be more accurate. See these women over here?" She points to a row of women along one wall. "They check all your work for mistakes. And remember, you should be doing about sixty address screens per hour," the supervisor said as she walked away. The last comment provided us with some merriment for the rest of the day as each of us temporaries took a turn sarcastically asking the others, "Did you get your sixty in this hour?"

Though we may have joked about these management production goals, we were not inattentive to them. We knew that our output and accuracy were being monitored.

Furthermore, billing requirements in some client companies, although ostensibly instituted to charge clients for the "true costs" of completing contracted work, also impose new constraints on workers. On a word processing assignment, for example, Patsy was required to keep a record of time spent on each task:

It's one of those places that handles work for people. It's like a secretarial service or something, where people who have businesses so small they can't hire their own secretarial support will send their work in to this place. You had to keep track of your time in six-minute intervals. So if I'd start typing a letter for someone. . . . They billed their clients by tenth of an hour. So then I'd have to write down, "This took me twelve minutes."

Information gathered for billing, however, may also be used to evaluate a worker's productivity (total volume of work produced, speed at particular tasks, or percentage of billable time).

Coverage Work and Control

Within fill-in or coverage work assignments temporaries were occasionally allowed greater autonomy than in routine work. Personal forms of supervision, like those between a secretary and her (or his) boss, often "imply a certain degree of flexibility in the pace and organization of work" (Glenn and Feldberg 1982, 210). Helen described working as a replacement secretary for a union umpire for a tin corporation:

I worked for an umpire for Agoff Tin. It was really neat. I would type up his decisions, which was very interesting. This guy gave me a lot of responsibility. He would say, "Just compose a letter to this guy and tell him what I think about this." And I typed up this letter, and he said, "Great." And he's a brilliant guy, too. I mean, I really respected him. So that was one of the best jobs I've ever had; it was much more challenging.

When temporaries were given the responsibility to grapple with a problem, the leeway to make decisions (even relatively minor or provisional ones), when their opinion or expertise was sought and valued in the completion of the work, the job was evaluated more favorably, and indeed temporaries applied themselves more fully to the tasks.

Coverage work assignments were not always free from pressure (for example, the boss might need a particular document produced quickly), but the stresses were not those of meeting production quotas. Whether temporaries in coverage work assignments, with a variety of less easily quantifiable tasks, applied enough effort is harder to assess. Temporary workers instead must discern and satisfy their immediate client company supervisor's expectations; professionally and cheerfully answering all telephone calls and completing requested work become salient markers of competent job performance. Successful temporaries quickly learned, however, that finishing the formal work tasks was often not enough. Temporaries must also appease their supervisors through demonstrating personal diligence and a strong work ethic regardless of the actual work load.

Mental Engagement

Like many other workers, temporaries wanted work that was meaningful, challenging, or allowed a sense of accomplishment. As Garson has noted: "Real work is a human need, perhaps right after the need for food and the need for love. It feels good to work well. But it feels bad to be used" (1975, 219). Temporary work, however, frequently did not satisfy workers' needs for meaningful employment.

Whether describing a routine or a coverage assignment, temporary workers often complained of boredom. No other theme was raised as consistently or as often. Indeed, from my first interview (incidentally conducted in Café Ennui) it became apparent that boredom was a significant issue for temporary workers. Temporaries were not using the term to describe a single dimension or aspect of their work, however. Boredom was variously used to indicate problems with the organization of the work (for example, variety and supply), a lack of meaning, and a lack of challenge or skill.

Routine Work and Relative Interest

Temporaries in routine clerical work assignments often complained quite bitterly about the boredom inherent in their plentiful yet unvarying supply of work, describing "piles," "stacks," "mountains," and "big drawers full of work" to be completed:

It was stacks of university applicants' applications. I
mean, they came in stacks in numerical order. And I just
had to take them off from a cart, unwrap the rubber
bands from them, and put them in filing drawers. It was
awful. Terribly mundane. (Ginny)

At one point I had to do this, like, this really horrible
project that really made me want to leave. I had to make,
like, duplicate files of these loans. And I mean it was just,
like, piles and piles. (Sergei)

Boredom in these assignments originated not with unoccupied time,
since the work was more than ample to fill the temporary's time, but
within the unvarying nature of the tasks themselves.

Additionally, it was difficult to find meaning or a sense of accomplishment in work when it was never finished, the end product was invisible,
or the context or purpose of the work was not understood. As Jackie
Krasas Rogers (1995, 146) has noted, the "temporary nature of the work
deprives the temporary of even the most limited realization of the finished product of her work. . . . Seldom do temporaries complete subsequent stages of a product that would provide them with a sense of
continuity."

Data entry, for example, reduced to the repetitive task of entering
information into the computer, requires little mental challenge, is never
finished, and provides only an anemic sense of accomplishment. For
example, I wrote in my field notes:

The supervisor comes over and gives me a packet of
three hundred address changes to be made. I get to work.
988765462. Transmit. Delete: 1550 Timber Oak Ln.
Type: 745 W. Lake Zurich Ave. Enter. Change city, zip
code, and phone number. Transmit. I do this four hundred fifty times during the first day. Included amidst the
address changes are twenty-six name changes, all
women—some have little cheery messages on the bill
stub like "Just married!!!!" Great. Happy for you. Your

> change of identity/name is providing dull, meaningless, spirit-sapping work for millions of people, mostly women, around the country. You should be proud. One form requested, "Please change 'Mrs.' to 'Ms.'" It was the highlight of an otherwise bleak day.
>
> I've been here three and a half weeks now making address changes for eight hours a day, five days a week. At approximately four hundred fifty address changes per day, I've made sure that about eighty-one hundred people won't miss their credit card bill.

The absence of mental challenge in data entry is a tribute or at least an indicator of the extent to which this particular segment of clerical work has been deskilled, routinized, and brought seamlessly under management's control. All knowledge and information necessary to complete the job is, presumably, possessed by management. For example, while on the data entry assignment described above, I observed a part-time clerical worker asking another employee a question. The supervisor rushed over and chastised her:

> "Why didn't you ask me first? You're not supposed to be bothering Julie. If you have a problem, you're supposed to ask me," the supervisor bitched.
>
> "I thought that . . . "
>
> "You're not paid to think. You are supposed to ask me if you have a problem!"

"You're not paid to think"—a phrase often heard in blue-collar and working-class jobs (Rubin 1976)—would have seemed out of place had this office not been so focused around essentially manual work.

Although thought had been largely removed from the work process, paradoxically much of the work required just enough mental attention to prevent daydreaming, conversing, or otherwise occupying time with one's own thoughts. Jon, for example, made the following observation in a comparison of data entry and reception work:

Another thing I hate doing is data entry. It bores me to tears. And the problem is with reception work you can be bored, but you can think about other things. You really don't have to engage your mind at all times. With data entry you have to be just paying enough attention to get the numbers right or the words right, to move through the fields the right way. So you can't think of other things. You can't turn your mind off. And that's one thing I hate about it.

Jon's assessment of data entry work mirrors the sentiments of an assembly-line worker interviewed by Ely Chinoy: "Most of the time you don't get a chance to think of anything. If you take your mind off what you're doing, you don't get the work done right" (Chinoy 1964, 57). The mind is engaged, but only at the most basic level; it is asked not to grapple with problems and questions, only to pick up bits of information long enough to guide the fingers to the appropriate keys (Braverman 1974). Data entry assignments, like manual assembly-line work, "require a high and continuous degree of mental attention without accompanying mental absorption" (Walker and Guest 1952, 40; see also Chinoy 1955, 1964).[3]

Coverage Work and Relative Interest

In fill-in or coverage work assignments the amount and type of work varies widely and somewhat unpredictably. On one secretarial and word processing assignment in December 1990, for example, I was kept busy with a variety of tasks from the moment I arrived until the moment I left. On another word processing assignment later that same month, however, looking busy was my central work challenge. My assigned tasks for the entire day—sending one four-page fax, taking eight brief telephone messages, typing three mailing labels, and word processing one three-line letter—cumulatively required less than an hour of on-task time. I wrote in my field notes, "Keeping myself busy seems to be the problem today. The morning was filled with various tasks (mine), but the afternoon is dragging. I just want the day to end."

Since temporaries rarely have the necessary organizational knowledge or autonomy to demonstrate initiative, they must rely on others, usually their client company supervisors, to regulate the flow of their work. If the phone is not ringing, the three-page memo the boss asked to have word processed two hours ago has been completed, and the supervisor is preoccupied or in a meeting, the temporary confronts a period of slack time.

Even when work tasks are clearly assigned at the beginning of the day, they often do not adequately occupy a temporary's time. Reception work, for example, is inherently unpredictable—the telephone rings off the hook or doesn't ring at all; the waiting area is filled with clients or empty: "At the university there were times when the day was sort of dragging. I knew what I was supposed to be doing, but the work was not ample. So I had a lot of time when I was sitting there" (Judy). Permanent workers are usually given an array of primary and secondary work tasks ensuring the relatively complete use of their time. The departmental receptionist may also handle supply requisitioning, light typing, or a variety of other sporadic jobs. A temporary worker filling in, particularly in the short term, is neither likely to be given these additional tasks nor familiar enough with the office's needs to be capable of anticipating them on his or her own. The difficulties of explaining work and the general lack of trust in temporaries' abilities (warranted or not) often meant that temporaries in coverage positions were given only the most minimal duties:

> The problem was that the job was a twofold thing and
> they didn't want to teach me everything because "you're
> only here two weeks and we just need this done. The rest
> of us will just do this." Well, they never taught me how
> to do it, so I never really learned the other half of the job.
> So it was, like, really horrible because I had nothing to
> do from, like, noon to four-thirty when I was supposed
> to leave. (Sergei)

Additionally, within coverage work, although it was more varied than routine jobs, many of the individual tasks still provided few mental challenges: "If you're just doing word processing . . . I mean, anyone can do that. If you're just typing . . . a lot of times they just want you to type in letters. That doesn't take a lot of talent. It tells you on the machine what to do anyway, so that's not difficult" (Lillian). Although word processing work was less routinized than data entry,[4] it was standardized to the point that many temporaries felt they were able to invest very little of themselves in the work.

Occasionally, coverage assignments provided more varied and interesting work. When a boss sought temporaries' opinions, gave temporaries responsibilities, or brought them into the work in the role of assistant, temps could find satisfaction in the work. Daniel described one of these assignments: "One time I worked at Pious University. That was nice. Computer stuff. You know, it was like a lot of research. The professor didn't want to have to take the time to be there, so it was, like, a lot of critical decisions. Well, not critical, but a lot of decisions that I had to make on my part." Similarly, Helen found a word processing assignment, where her opinion was solicited and valued, both challenging and interesting: "They literally said, 'If there's anything that you think that a lay person would find totally cryptic,' because the document was for lay people, 'let us know. And if you see any grammar things, fix it.' That was really interesting, too. It would be a lot more challenging. That's really rare. That's really, really rare." Coverage assignments did not always provide more interesting work, but the possibility of more varied challenging tasks existed in these less fragmented and routinized positions.

Sociability

Sociability with others at work can make seemingly intolerable jobs tolerable and average jobs enjoyable. Ethnographic studies of work document high levels of worker dissatisfaction and boredom (Chinoy 1955, 1964; Crozier 1971; Garson 1975; Kanter 1977; Cockburn 1983; Westwood 1984; Cockburn 1985; Garson 1988). Yet many of these same studies show how workers, through informal work groups, shopfloor culture, and friendship networks, derived enjoyment and satisfaction from their work lives. Sallie Westwood noted in her study of women factory workers:

> Friendships were an essential and vital part of life on the
> shopfloor; they made work tolerable and at times even
> fun. Friends were the major antidote to the pressures of
> work: "Well, we don't like the work that much, but we
> don't like to move around either. You get friends here
> who keep you going, so you say, 'It's not so bad, really.'"
> (1984, 90)

Similarly, as one man in Cynthia Cockburn's study of workers in a
garment factory put it, "Going to work, with people, that was the thing,
rather than working" (1985, 67).

Besides ameliorating the stresses of work, adding meaning to a work
life otherwise bereft of personal significance, friendships at work can
provide a sense of belonging, self-worth, and shared values (Fischer
1982; Rubin 1986; Nardi 1992). Furthermore, the importance of a work
network, both on and off the job, can be seen clearly in the many
negative effects resulting from its loss among other groups of workers.
Unemployed workers, for example, experience a precipitous rise in both
mental and physical illnesses after the loss of their jobs (Bluestone and
Harrison 1982; Bensman and Lynch 1987).

Temporaries valued work settings that provided the opportunity for
sociability with others on the job. Indeed, temporaries reserved their
harshest evaluations for assignments that offered (or "permitted") the
fewest chances for socializing. Patsy, for example, decried the lack of
social opportunities at one of her placements: "Oh, it was awful, just
awful. And one of those places where no one smiles, no one talks, and no
one has lunch together. Like, noon comes and they just scatter like rats.
And then they come back at one o'clock."

While some temporaries interpreted the lack of social embeddedness
as an advantage of the work, being able to sidestep office politics and gossip (Olesen and Katsuranis 1978; McNally 1979), most were ambivalent:

> It is kind of bleak in that respect. I mean, you're always
> marginal. You're totally peripheral. You're not part of
> anything. I mean, I'm kind of glad that I'm not part of

the office politics, because when you're on an assignment
for two or three weeks sometimes things start to surface.
You'll pick up on certain feuds going on in the office.
And I'm really overjoyed that I get to leave after three
weeks. I don't have to be a part of that. (Helen)

Freedom, in other words, is a double-edged sword.

For many temporaries, the most telling symptom of a work life deficient in sociability is the lack of lunch-time companions. Whereas permanent workers have their regular lunch partners and habits, temporaries must negotiate anew, on each assignment, their lunch routine. As
Helen noted, "The life of the temp is, you know, eating lunch alone
every single day." Kimberly made a similar complaint: "There was another temp there, so she and I would talk to each other. But I had to
cover the phones when the other temp went to lunch, and she'd cover
when I went to lunch. And sitting in the cafeteria alone is not a fun part
of temping." A new full-time employee on his or her first days, regardless
of organizational position, would be looked after, introduced to other
employees, and invited to socialize. Temporaries, however, are often left
to fend for themselves.[5]

Additionally, because almost all the other employees, including those
at nominally the same level, consider themselves in a supervisory or
quasi-supervisory role above temporaries (Olesen and Katsuranis 1978;
Parker 1994), the possibility of forming equal-status relationships in the
workplace is difficult. On one of my assignments Beverly, my helpful co-
worker, was an additional source of anxiety rather than a workplace
friend:

> Beverly was on my case all day long. Telling me what I
> did wrong with each call. Listening. Hovering. Ready to
> turn me in for the slightest offense. But I thanked her for
> her "help" and "advice" profusely, hoping my insincerity
> wasn't showing—"Beverly, I really don't give a shit about
> this job. You've obviously mistaken me for someone who
> gives a damn."

The quality of office-based relationships may be further damaged by stereotypes of temporaries as less committed, less qualified, and less principled workers. In sum, the worker who is believed socially deficient is not sought out for friendship.

Routine Work and Sociability

When work is highly routinized and structured, like most temporary work, the opportunities for meaningful social interaction on the job are even further diminished. As Glenn and Feldberg have pointed out, "These [work] arrangements are defended on the grounds of efficiency. However, they also limit workers' opportunities to form face-to-face relationships with other workers" (1982, 215). Sometimes the work was so rigidly structured that, after being shown to their work area by a supervisor, temporaries reported interacting with no one else during the entire assignment. Within many routine placements temporaries are required to interact with a computer (or a file cabinet) rather than other workers to complete their assigned tasks.[6] During one four-week data entry assignment, for example, I shared only the briefest of nonverbal interactions with one of my nearest co-workers:

> One of the regular staff, who sat directly across from me (our toes almost touching underneath the back-to-back work stations), smiled at me briefly once as she repeatedly spoke into her headset. "Number and amount please. The transaction number is. . . . " No one else bothered. Sometimes it started to sound like she was saying, "Cover your mouth please." I liked that. It broke the monotony.

My field notes for this assignment record only a few lines of conversation with other workers followed by the observation, "These were the only people I spoke to all day, and then only briefly, before the disapproving gaze of the supervisor from her perch at the front of the 'assembly line' wandered our way."

Moreover, since time away from one's assigned work area is both highly visible and highly discouraged, temporaries rarely get to see workers in other parts of the company. As one temp on a data entry assignment noted, "I had hoped to see more of how the company worked, but we're really isolated from the rest of the company" (Judy). Without either the occasion to circulate or the rationale of task-related interactions, the opportunity to meet other employees, find out about their jobs, or simply share a laugh are stifled. Sociability, to the extent that it occurs at all in these settings, is squeezed out or stolen while supervisors are looking the other way.

Coverage Work and Sociability

Opportunities and occasions to interact with others on the job are somewhat greater within coverage work assignments. Helen outlined her time spent on a favorable departmental secretarial assignment:

> I was in their what-ja-ma-call-it department. It was polymers and it was like some . . . I don't know what they do, but they work keeping millions of Americans happy. No complaints, nothing. They were really happy with me. I had a blast. People were really nice. There was a fair amount of stuff to do. It was mostly phones. It paid well. So, it was okay, wasn't bad. And that's my ideal assignment.

During the course of a typical work day temporaries in a coverage assignment may be called on to communicate and interact with their principal boss, mail delivery clerks, office guests, telephone callers, or other secretaries. Though these relationships may not run deep, sharing a piece of office gossip, talking about a recent movie, or even discussing the weather has its rewards.

Aleshia, working as a replacement secretary/receptionist in a small architectural firm, described how her co-workers included her in their socializing and gossip circles. During their informal talk she had discussed her interest and degree in Russian history. A co-worker gave her a romance novel with a Russian motif: "Peggy gave me a book about . . . it was a Harlequin romance-type book. You know, like *Princess Daisy* or something like that? But a big long one. And it was about Russia instead of being the southern belle. And I don't read those books, generally. But it was a nice gesture, really." The action revealed the extent to which Aleshia had become known as an individual to her co-workers. In routinized work the possibility that one's co-workers could have garnered enough personal information or formed close enough feelings to offer even a token gift was extremely unlikely.

The Paradox of Time

The work experience of a clerical temporary employee is also affected by the variable temporal length of assignments and movement through a number of placements and organizations. Some analysts have argued, "Numerous work assignments and roles offer temporary employees highly varied circumstances, in contrast to the homogeneous world of the clerk on a continuing job" (Olesen and Katsuranis 1978, 334; see also McNally 1979). Many of the temporaries I interviewed also mentioned this aspect of their work: at least they, unlike permanent employees, could move on:

> Just changing scenery makes it a little more palatable. At
> least you're constantly changing your location and stuff. I
> guess that's a little better. Something new, I guess. I
> thank God I get to leave. The people who work there
> full-time are so miserable. At least I can walk away. It's
> not that much of an improvement, but it helps. (Helen)

Like the relief man on the assembly line (Walker and Guest 1952; Chinoy 1964), the temporary worker may experience more variety in his or her work life than the permanent, single-task employee.

Reintegration or reinvigoration of work through horizontal mobility, however, may be relatively superficial. Many routine office tasks given to temps, after all, are essentially the same across organizations: filing and data entry are filing and data entry wherever they are done. Though it may be interesting to "change scenery," working in a different building or a different part of town, the rapid change of work setting comes at a high cost. Frequent changes hamper a temporary worker's opportunities to develop even a modicum of trust and autonomy, more varied or interesting work tasks, and stable work groups.[7] Like Helen, many temporaries expressed an ambivalence toward greater variety through horizontal mobility.

Whether the impermanence of the work was seen as a benefit or a detriment depended on the qualities of any particular placement. If the work was tedious and disliked, the unpleasantness could be ameliorated by the shortness of duration. If the work was liked, however, it could become even better over time. And time, at least on some fill-in or coverage assignments, not only increased predictability but also could increase the level of autonomy, the intrinsic interest of the work, and social possibilities.

Routine Work and Time

Not surprisingly, temporaries doing routine work valued the rapid change of assignments. Judy, for example, noted that, given the kind of work she usually received, the shorter the duration, the better: "I think I prefer the short-time assignments, unless, of course, I was doing something I liked. I like the accounting better than, let's say, the data entry." Indeed, temporaries often noted that the work was tolerable only because it was short-term and they could anticipate its end: "I'm the type of person that if I do a job, I want to do it. And I want to be challenged. So all of these assignments have been really sort of easy for me. But I try not to let that bother me because I know it's not something I'm going to stay with, especially the one-day things" (Mike). Within routine assignments, in which the work has been organizationally and structurally impoverished, increased time on the job cannot significantly overcome its deficits and may only make the work seem more monotonous and tedious. Short-term work at least means temporaries get to move on quickly, chasing an ever-elusive, desirable, and rewarding assignment.

Coverage Work and Time

Long tenure can overcome at least some of the deficiencies of the work within coverage assignments. Bobby Jean described how her responsibilities and the variety of her assigned tasks increased over time on a long-term coverage assignment:

> Most places don't expect too much out of you in the beginning. And then it's kind of nice to prove yourself and they give you more responsibility. And they like you that much more. The girl that I was replacing was on maternity leave for, like, six months. As I got more familiar with the job, they kept giving me more responsibility. And part of it was to wheel and deal with students about their tuition payments, to make payment arrangements with them.

Bobby Jean took great pride in helping a student whose economic situation had dramatically declined secure financial aid to continue his studies. Similarly, Lillian described how her comfort level and her opportunities for sociability grew with tenure:

> In one respect long-term assignments are nicer because I know all the people there. I know how the system works. I know what papers you have to fill in, what you have to do, what's expected of you. So that's nice. You know where you're going. And there's not going to be any big surprises like, "Oh, what am I going to be doing today? What type of environment is it going to be?"

Familiarity and trust accumulated over time on coverage assignments, then, may reinvigorate the work—at least up to the full-time or permanent level of that position.

Furthermore, relatively long tenure allowed temporaries to form relationships with their co-workers and office mates. Ruby described relatively extensive integration into work groups and sociability networks during a temporary assignment of several months:

> On long-term assignments you don't have to move around so much. You can adjust to people. You can make friends. The short-term assignments, you really don't get time to make friends. So I think a long-term assignment gives you time to get familiar with the person and get real comfortable where you can talk. On short-term assignments I really don't make friends or say too much of anything. I just do my job and take lunch maybe by myself. And walk out and come on back.

Linda noted a similar increase in sociability and social integration into the workplace: "I spent about six weeks at one place last summer. That was pretty good because you get to know people and they get to know you. And they start treating you like a real person." An extended assignment of several weeks or months within a single client company clarifies and legitimates the temporaries' presence and organizational role and allows or encourages integration into existing work and friendship groups.[8] Temporaries who are around long enough to be seen as individuals may be treated more respectfully and allowed greater autonomy and initiative.

Conclusion

Although managers may believe that enhancing their control over the work process and the temporary worker increases efficiency and profitability, these efforts frequently have serious negative consequences for both workers and management.[9] Workers with autonomy can take pride or find personal fulfillment using judgment, finding solutions, or completing a product or job. Intensive formal control removes temporary employees' personal motivation, commitment, and loyalty and creates workers who "work to the rule" or "put in the required number of hours . . . to do only their defined tasks, regardless of the organization's needs" (Glenn and Feldberg 1982, 211). Furthermore, when the balance of control shifts to management, work becomes something to be endured. No longer capable of providing a sense of fulfillment or a sense of self, work becomes debilitating and a painful reminder of one's place in the world.

5 *Playing the Part*

The average person will form his judgment of the company through his contact with one individual. If this person is rude or inefficient, it will require a lot of courtesy and efficiency to overcome the bad impression. Every member of an organization who in any capacity comes in contact with the public is a salesman . . . the impression he makes is an advertisement . . . good or bad. (Right Temporaries, Inc., *What Does Right Temporaries, Inc. Expect of Me?*)

The good thing about temping is that you really learned a lot of professional skills, I think—just how to behave in an office. (Natalie)

Successful temporaries must be able to do more than produce the required work; they must also exhibit "professionalism," or "look and play the part." Such temporaries know how to dress in the proper white-collar costume (do "gender-appropriate corporate drag"), adopt a suitable demeanor (with an appropriate mix of cooperative deference and cheer), and demonstrate personal diligence and a strong work ethic regardless of the actual work load (look busy). Although these impression management abilities are recognized and demanded as part of proper job performance, they are not formally compensated by the temporary industry.

Temporary agencies tend to favor workers who exhibit these characteristics at the outset, but the agencies do not surrender the definition of "professional conduct" to the individual's judgment. Recognizing that their reputation depends on the conduct of the temporaries they send out, agencies maintain control over the definition of professional behavior and attempt to impose as much uniformity as possible over the appearance, attitudes, and behaviors of their temporary staff.[1] The temporary who does not play the part appropriately, regardless of his or her abilities to complete the formal work tasks, will not survive long in the temporary industry.

Impression Management and Emotional Labor

Temporaries are implored to perform impression management and emotional labor as part of proper job performance. At the time of registration temporaries are screened or auditioned for impression management (Goffman 1959) and emotional labor skills (Hochschild 1983), a level of "professionalism," in the vernacular of the temporary industry.[2] Their clothing, their punctuality for agency appointments, and how they handle themselves in one-on-one interactions with temporary counselors are all used as indicators of "success" on assignment (Moore 1963, 36; Gottfried 1992; Parker 1994).

Beginning at registration, temporaries are advised and socialized, formally and informally, to conform to the agency's standards of professionalism. Typing and word processing practice copy and tests, for example, are not randomly chosen pieces of text devoid of ideological content. Copy material is tailored to emphasize and instill in temporaries the attitudes and behaviors the agency desires. The practice typing copy at the time I registered, for example, included this emotional labor edict: "The receptionist should have an outgoing personality and a sunny disposition." A temporary at one agency reported that "her orientation and training consisted mostly of socialization—learning how to become a model 'temp,' how to groom and dress, and what attitudes and behaviors were becoming of a temporary worker" (9 to 5 1986, 28).[3]

Some prospective temporaries may be naive enough to think that they are just taking a typing test and registering, but they are indeed interviewing and auditioning. Wendy, a temporary counselor, noted that evaluations of temporaries' appearance and behavior were considered in scheduling work assignments: "If it's working for an advertising agency or it's a real corporate environment, they have to look nice and all that. I mean, you don't want to send somebody who's not articulate to be a switchboard operator." Looking "nice" actually refers to a whole constellation of behaviors and attitudes the temporary must possess, learn, or be able to "put on" at the appropriate time. Temporary positions, then, are assigned based on these additional "professional" or impression management abilities.

At the agency where I did the majority of my field work, appropriate behavior was positively sanctioned with formal thank-you cards. Favorable quality control reports were photocopied, attached to half of a thank-you card, and sent to temporaries with a handwritten but unvarying message: "Thank you so much for doing such a wonderful job. We appreciate your professionalism and hard work. Thanks again for being the best!" Correspondingly, "unprofessional" behavior met with negative sanctions through more formal one-on-one "counseling" sessions between the errant temporary and his or her temporary counselor, through termination of the assignment, or through work deprivation.

Looking the Part

Successful temporary workers, like white-collar workers in general, must know how to dress in the appropriate white-collar costumes. Indeed, appearance for temporary workers may at times be more important for securing assignments than ability. Moore, for example, noted, "At some places, attractiveness may offset deficiencies in ability, while at others ability is the only criterion" (Moore 1963, 141). A 1986 study of the temporary industry found a similar emphasis on looks: a receptionist at one temporary agency reported filing "evaluation cards of temporary worker applicants that had comments like 'homely' and 'stunning' written on them with virtually no mention of office skills" (9 to 5 1986, 28–29).

The importance of appearance in the temporary industry also became evident during the course of my study. Agency literature frequently emphasized "good grooming, cleanliness, and accepted standards of business dress" (Right Temporaries, Inc. 1989b, 9). Temporary workers were advised to observe and conform to each client company's standard of dress. Agencies emphasized that making these fine discriminations and "fitting in" were expected aspects of proper job performance: "Generally, professional attire is always appropriate the first day. Take a cue from the others in the office; if more casual attire is permitted, feel free to dress so" (Right Temporaries, Inc. 1989b, 7). During scheduling calls temporary counselors often included a brief description of the work environment ("It's very corporate" or "It's small and casual") and implicit or verbalized instructions about appropriate attire ("You should wear a skirt" or "Shirt, tie, and khakis are adequate").

What to wear to work was, indeed, a routine and frequently troubling problem for temporary workers. Most permanent workers also adjust their work wardrobes to specific company cultures, but they typically do this only once, when they first hire on (acquiring, for example, the informally required pinstripe suits, white shirts, and silk ties). Temporary workers, however, must make these fine discriminations and adjustments in their appearance every time they go on a new assignment, sometimes several times a month. Kara, for example, articulated the complexity and variability of the decision making required for "dressing for success" on each new assignment:

> You'd feel it out, because you'd wear something one day and then you'd realize, "Whoa, it's way too dressy!" You don't have to get that dressed up for this company. Like if they'd say lawyer's office. I'd say, "Do I have to wear a suit?" And the temporary counselor would sometimes

say, "Yes." For an envelope-stuffing assignment, I said,
"Am I going to be out in the open? Do I have to wear
something nice? Or can I just wear pants?" And she said,
"Oh yeah. I think you're probably going to be in the
back of the office." So I'd just wear pants. But I never
wear jeans to something like that.

Connie employed another common strategy of initially erring on the
formal side (possibly spending a day uncomfortably overdressed) and
modifying and conforming to the client company norms on subsequent
days of the assignment: "The first day would always be professional. I
would always wear a suit the first day. And then from then on I would
say, 'Oh, I could wear my slacks.' But that first day would always be in a
professional suit." Informal abilities of observation and discrimination,
then, were necessary aspects of performing the impression management
that was required of temporary employees. As in the theater, successful
temporaries knew that an inappropriate costume could cause their performance to falter even when it was otherwise credible.

In temporary work the importance of appearance to a credible performance became particularly visible when minor dress code infractions
met with negative social sanctions. Helen, for example, reported that she
received formal complaints about her appearance and in the end believed
that client companies valued physical appearance over productive ability:
"It's, like, don't you care that you have a very educated, professional
person? Professional sounding, you know? And somebody so efficient?
And literate? Doesn't that count for anything? Isn't that the important
thing here? And then you realize, no. Dress is more important than
output." Others reported similar complaints regarding their personal
appearance, complaints they felt were intrusive, irrational, and irrele-
vant. Though these temporaries rarely received criticism about their
work per se, their performance of the temporary role faltered in the
wardrobe and makeup departments.

A credible performance demanded attire that was not only "professional" but also gender-appropriate. Male and female temporaries, like
male and female office workers generally, were held to different standards

of dress. Typically, gender-differentiating clothing such as neckties for men and skirts for women were informally or formally required. Judy, for example, noted: "I have to wear a dress or a suit every day. Okay? At Midwestern Bank the women are not allowed to wear slacks. We were told from the beginning that slacks were not allowed." In addition, differential regulations about acceptable hairstyles, makeup, and jewelry were sometimes informally enforced. The proper enactment of gender, then, was intertwined with the proper performance of the temporary role. Whereas female temporaries were expected to model their appearances after full-time female secretaries, male temporaries, often lacking similar-status males to model, were expected to blend in with higher-status men.

The task of fitting in for male temporaries was complicated by the feminine stage settings in which they often performed their temporary roles. I described one of my work areas, a rather typical temporary work setting, as follows:

> I am at Cindy's work station: a small stuffed dog with a green plastic heart-shaped nose, a plastic gumball machine (empty), candy jar, a "Handle with Care" button, two photographs of young black children (boy pictured in basketball uniform; girl pictured in kitchen with plastic stethoscope), two bookmarks pinned up—one with a rainbow-and-daisies pattern reads, "Every Day Is a New Gift from God"; the other is "Murphy's Laws."

An extra pair of pumps stashed underneath the desk, pinup photographs on the walls, and other personal or "feminine" territorial markers often visually announced the incongruous presence of a man. Male temporaries, already risking their status as "real" men through violating the implicit sexual division of labor (Pringle 1988, 80), were consequently held to high standards of masculine attire.

Male temporaries' gender crossing, or violation of the boundary between "women's work" and "men's work," was recognized, highlighted, and partially neutralized through a series of recurrent jokes. One joke, which I heard to the point of annoyance, played on themes of mistaken identity and gender reversal. Full-time workers, noticing a male temporary for the first time, would declare with mock seriousness, "Why, (Marcia, Faye, Lucy), you've changed!" Another common joke was knowingly to misattribute ownership of a full-time female employee's personal, "feminine" trappings to the male temporary through a mock compliment such as, "Nice pumps." Such jokes provided male temporaries the opportunity to assert their masculinity, countering the visual appearance of being out of place and thus restoring temporarily threatened meanings of masculinity and femininity in both the workplace and the wider society (see Spradley and Mann 1975).

Besides formal sanctions (such as face-to-face confrontations with client supervisors or temporary counselors) regarding deviations from gendered and professional personal appearances, temporaries were occasionally alerted to "deficient" appearance or attire through more subtle means:

> I've never gotten any grief from the agency about my appearance. But they have once or twice sent me the back of the client evaluation, and I've always noticed that the personal appearance is always the middle. Average. Yeah, for the other things it will always be, like, the five or the *A* or whatever it is. But for personal appearance I'm always a three or a four. (Patsy)

Exposure to client company evaluations, an askance look from a supervisor, an overheard comment from a co-worker, or other informal sanctions while in the workplace may alert temporaries to disapproval regarding their personal appearance.

Such disapproval concerning attire or appearance was recognized by many temporary workers, but even when they were willing to conform, they often did not have the resources to meet the client company's standard of dress. Yet, like transportation costs, procuring a proper wardrobe is presumed to be the responsibility of individual workers. Ruby, for example, although economically struggling, was able to press her church clothing into corporate service with minimal additional financial outlay:

I have dress clothes to wear to work. So that wasn't a
problem—what I'm going to put on to go to work. Because, like I told you, because of my going to religious
meetings and things I have to have dress wear. So I have
clothes and stuff already. Just different stockings. Different colored stockings and stuff. As long as I can afford
the stockings, I have the clothes to go with it.

Mike was able to supplement an existing work wardrobe, although not
without kin assistance, to meet client company dress regulations:

Since I've been in banking for a while I had to look half-
way decent so . . . plus my father knows people, so he got
me a suit, another suit besides this one. So I do okay.
Nobody ever says I look bad, so I figure I'm doing okay.
The only thing I've had to buy is socks and a couple of
ties, because I want them. So I've been lucky in the
wardrobe department.

Old, new, borrowed, or stolen, appropriate corporate wear must be
found and worn by all workers, temporary or not. This employer expectation of a "corporate look," although occasionally creating economic
hardship, was generally accepted by the temporaries I interviewed.

Even temporaries who lacked suitable work clothing at the beginning
of their temporary stint often accepted an employer's right to determine and enforce the definition of appropriate attire. These temporaries
quickly had to piece together a minimally adequate wardrobe, sometimes at the open request of client company supervisors:

I know that one of the other temps at Midwestern Bank
didn't have a suit. And when our supervisor laid down
the law the first day. . . . He told us about the laws of
wearing our jackets here, there, and everywhere. This kid
raised his hand and said, "I don't have a suit." It almost

looked like the supervisor was going to say, "Well, get out of here." And the supervisor said, "Well, can you get one?" And the kid was, like, "Yeah, I guess so." So he has one suit, one white shirt, and one tie. And we've been on this assignment for more than two months. (Mike)[4]

I too was asked to obtain a blazer for a particular temporary assignment: the client had decided that my usual corporate outfit of loafers, khakis, shirt, and tie did not project the professional image the organization desired. A full-time employee may find such a request reasonable (or at least be willing to acquiesce in the interest of long-term employment or advancement), but a temporary worker has a very different incentive structure for making major personal expenditures at the request of a client company supervisor. The cost of a blazer, even an inexpensive one, was a personal budgetary burden.

Some temporaries pursue strategies that minimize the exploitation or expense of compliance. Patsy described her economically creative wardrobe acquisition and maintenance strategies:

> I pick up whatever is on sale. What I wear to work, I
> would never wear at any other time in my life. If I find a
> skirt someplace for ten bucks, I buy it. I'm not going to
> spend a lot of money on this. I would not wear a suit on
> a temporary assignment because it's really dirty work. I
> mean, you're always getting ink and toner and White-
> out on your clothes. I have a couple of suits, but I guess
> I'm not going to wear them. Who knows when I'll be in
> a position to buy another suit. So I wear them when I go
> to apply for temporary work. And then the rest of the
> time, you know, cheap old blouses and skirts.

Joanne, anticipating work wardrobe inquiries, provided an elaborate explanation for each article of clothing in the work outfit she was wearing the day of our interview:

> I thought you would ask me how do I budget myself
> working like this, as far as clothes and that. I get it from
> the secondhand store. And if you know where to shop
> and how to shop, you get away like a bandit. Matter of
> fact, everything I have on today I . . . the necklace was
> ninety-nine cents. The earrings were forty-nine cents.
> The skirt was a dollar and a half. The jacket was about
> seventy-five cents or a dollar. And the blouse was about a
> dollar and a half. My shoes I got at Payless for, like, nine
> dollars. There's a way you can dress and look like an ex-
> ecutive. And look rich, but you don't have to pay. You
> know, you can dress like champagne money for beer
> money.

Like homemakers who stretch inadequate family budgets by increasing their labor in the "private sphere" (Luxton 1980), temporary workers minimize the hidden expenses of acquiring and maintaining a work wardrobe by careful budgeting and shopping.

This close attention to temporaries' physical appearance by both agencies and client companies is often offensive and humiliating to temporary workers. It highlights not only their subordinate position within the work world but their assumed subordinate position within the society at large, and it implies that temporaries are inherently deficient in personal judgment, taste, and character. Like stereotypes of the poor as "dirty," temporaries' financial difficulties of appearing white-collar are obscured behind presumptions of social ineptitude and personal failure.

Additionally, the right to dictate or define appropriate appearance increases client companies' control over temporary workers. Greta Foff Paules (1991), in her study of waitresses, noted the function of their uniforms:

> While the waitress's maidlike uniform functions to di-
> minish her status, . . . the executive's "uniform" is de-
> signed for status enhancement. . . . The uniform of the
> executive . . . differs from that of the service worker in

> that it is at least ostensibly voluntary, indicating that
> however strictly the businessperson's appearance is con-
> trolled by her work, this control is not recognized as a
> right. (136)

Like waitresses, military personnel, and prisoners, temporaries are expected to forfeit personal control over their appearance to management.
This loss of autonomy accentuates a sense of powerlessness that can be
used by management to gain compliance, conformity, and control.

An emphasis on appropriate work attire also ensures that temporaries
do not distract from or disrupt the office landscape, that they "fit in."
Temporaries may be required to fit in to maintain discipline among full-
time workers. As Judy commented: "People who usually work downtown at a big company or whatever, they dress their best. So we have to
keep up with that thing." Company rules and norms (dress codes, hours
of operation, appropriate levels of output or effort, and the like) must be
observed by everyone for the company to maintain the legitimacy of
these claimed privileges or areas of control. Allowing anyone, even a
temporary worker, to break the rules may start the company management down a slippery slope of lost control and discipline.

Agencies and client companies have vested interests in temporary
workers' expending part of their wage packet to keep up appearances,[5]
but temporary employees often have quite different budgetary priorities.
Daniel, for example, spoke about the tensions between his client company's interests and his own:

> They always harass me at Benefit Insurance because I
> just wear sweater and slacks or slacks and a shirt. And
> they say to me, "Why don't you wear a suit?" I said, "You
> pay me suit money, I'll wear a suit." But I'm not going to
> wear a suit or something really good to be sitting here,
> crawling on the floor with files or whatever. Just to get a
> white shirt cleaned is two dollars and fifty cents. And I'm
> going to have five of those done, and you're only paying
> me six dollars, seven dollars an hour?! Give me a break.

Similarly, Helen questioned what was a reasonable expenditure for temporary work clothing:

> I had been looking around for clothes, and you can't find a woman's dress, like a conservative woman's dress, new, under a hundred something, even on sale. I want to blow my paycheck on some little fou-fou dress? I mean, come on! How much are you supposed to pump into this? I'm, like, what about attitude? I think I do an excellent job. I think I'm very meticulous. I rarely get something handed back for corrections. You know, I'm really careful. I'm really good on the phone. And I think I do the best job that anybody can do.

Though client companies have fundamentally altered the employer-employee relationship, they have not modified their expectations: they want well-dressed, committed workers. Yet just as client companies avoid investing resources (training, benefits, wages, and so on) in their short-term employees, temporaries resist investing their scarce resources in short-term employers. Consequently, conflicts over appearance and attire, rather than simple pettiness or a trivial sideline, may be one form of temporary worker resistance.

Looking Submissive

Looking submissive or adopting a suitable demeanor with an appropriate mix of cooperation, deference, and cheer was essential for the successful performance of the temporary role and was expected and demanded by temporary agencies: "A cooperative, friendly attitude makes you an invaluable employee—and our customer, a satisfied one!" (Right Temporaries, Inc. 1989b). Like many service workers, temporaries were expected to "put on a happy face" whether or not they were particularly happy.

Although the outward appearance of pleasantness, like the smile of the flight attendant, is generally acceptable for a client company's clients, a more convincing act is often required to create the desired emotional state in client company supervisors or personnel. To this end, temporary agencies, like the airlines, urged deep acting techniques (Hochschild 1983) on their temporary workers. Temporaries were instructed to think of themselves as "guests" rather than laborers engaged in a primarily economic transaction: "Try to remember that you are a guest in each new office and must always observe the basic rules of etiquette" (Right Temporaries, Inc. 1989b). Drawing on their personal knowledge of behavior appropriate to a well-behaved guest, temporaries were expected to avoid potentially conflict-laden behaviors or topics. Borrowing money, smoking, or discussing taboo subjects such as pay rates, office politics, or sexual behavior while on the job were specifically forbidden (Right Temporaries, Inc. 1989c). A polite guest, temporaries are reminded, neither challenges nor otherwise risks offending his or her host.

Notably, temporary agencies and airlines used the same social situation—a social visit—as the metaphor on which to base standards for their employees' behavior. Whereas temporary agencies emphasized adopting the "guest" role, airlines stressed the "host" role for their employees, encouraging flight attendants to think of the airplane cabin as their "living room" and to deal with customers as if they were kith or kin (Hochschild 1983). Both roles imply being on one's best behavior and putting others' feelings first.

The guest metaphor, moreover, quickly renders inappropriate any complaining or self-assertion by temporary workers on assignment. The commercial nature of the relationship is obscured by the personal relations fiction, and criticisms about the rate of pay, work tasks, or working conditions are defined as outside the boundaries of legitimate conversation: "Please do . . . observe the hours, procedures, and work methods of the customers without criticism" (Right Temporaries, Inc. 1989b). Yet complaints and criticisms do arise. Temporaries are instructed to bring these work-related problems to the attention of their agency rather than the client company. The temporary agency, in turn, rather than directly addressing the source of the conflict, often simply applies further pressure or emotional management techniques to bring the individual temporary's anger boundaries into line with the agency's, to discount or reframe almost all grievances as without merit.

Temporaries, then, learn that they must shift their personal anger boundaries (Hochschild 1983) and engage in emotional labor to disguise or manage their feelings to ensure access to work. Shelley, for example, reported an incident in which she failed to adopt the appropriate submissive and apologetic demeanor, to play the role of polite guest, in the face of hostile behavior from the client:

> I was getting something and I closed this door hard. It was clearly an accident, but this woman starts yelling at me about it. And I told her, "I really don't appreciate the way you're talking to me. It's obvious that it was an accident. And I find it insulting that you feel you need to say something." Well, she went away and called my agency and lied. Said that I had been very rude to her and demanding that they ask me to apologize. The company even threatened to cancel the entire account unless I apologized. Can you believe that? So my agency calls and asks me to apologize to this woman for them. Now I don't like being put in that kind of situation. She certainly didn't deserve an apology from me; she owed me one. But I did. I apologized, sort of. I told her in a way that she felt that I had apologized, but that I could live with.

Shelley also acknowledged that she began tolerating more "garbage" on the job in order to safeguard her income:

> I have had men try to call me "honey" or "darling" and I won't take that. I won't take that or any innuendoes at all. I tell them, "My name is Shelley or Ms. Cunningham, whichever you prefer." But there are times when you put up with more garbage. If things are real

lean, I'll put up with a lot more on a job. But I won't put up with that at all. "My name is Shelley or Ms. Cunningham." That's one thing I won't put up with.

There were also pressures on temporaries to perform as if they were "one of the family" when dealing with the client company's customers. A telephone caller, for example, should be serviced by the temporary worker as if everything were "business as usual." The temporary's temporary status should remain concealed:

> Someone calls and says, "Let me talk to Ron Smith."
> Like Ron Smith is a very well known guy and I should
> know who Ron Smith is. I think it looks bad for the
> company for this temp to say, "Well, I don't know who
> Ron Smith is, can you wait a minute while I look in my
> directory? I'm a temp." I always interrupt people. I'll just
> go knock on the door if I don't know, because I think I'm
> better off doing that. (Mary)

Temporaries frequently lacked the organizational knowledge to perform this aspect of their role convincingly. Not only did they not recognize everyone or know the business well enough; full-time workers rarely felt compelled to provide adequate information to the temporary. Supervisors, for example, often neglected to inform lower-status temporaries about their comings and goings—crucial information for the successful performance of reception duties:

> Actually, I think the worst thing is the phones, because
> you don't know anything about the people in the company. It just amazes me that people assign you to answer
> phones. Where there's important people needing to get
> these calls and they want them handled right, yet there's
> just no way you can do it. You just don't have the information. Well, you need to know the hierarchical setup.
> Is this the boss calling or is this the major client calling?

And people tend not to tell you where they are, because
they don't see you as their regular secretary. People who
call in expect you to know everything and you don't
know anything! They get upset. It's ridiculous, and it's
not good for the company. (Linda)

Temporaries, then, frequently were required to perform improvisation-
ally, creating appropriate, businesslike explanations for the absence of
full-time workers ("I'm sorry. He's in a meeting right now. May I take a
message?").

Additionally, temporaries were expected, like flight attendants and
full-time secretaries, to suppress their anger with "irates." As gatekeepers,
temporaries often had to perform "front work" (Kanter 1977) for their
supervisors and manage the anger of callers denied access to more power-
ful, higher-status individuals or apologize, admitting inadequacy, for not
having even the most basic information the caller is requesting. Frequently, temporaries were also ritually expected to accept blame for
others' inadequate work performances ("Oh, I hate it too when you hear
people on the phone, 'Oh, things didn't go right? Oh, well . . . we have a
temp this week.' And you know you're doing excellent work for the
situation." [Linda]).

Temporaries, like secretaries in general (Benet 1972; Kanter 1977;
Pringle 1988), are also expected to adopt a deferential stance toward
management and supervisors. Indeed, many secretarial tasks require
temporaries physically to "sit at attention" before superordinates. This
deference is also deeply gendered. Women in American culture generally
have been expected to take submissive, often self-effacing, and subordinate roles vis-à-vis men, and the sexual division of labor within the office
seems to demand, much to the chagrin of many female temporaries, the
(re)enactment of these traditional gender roles: "I also resent the fact that
usually a man wants me to sit in front of him and take dictation when he
could pick up something like this tape recorder and dictate into a machine and just give me the tape. Why do I have to sit here and then sit
down and transcribe? It's very inefficient" (Mary). As Kathy E. Ferguson
points out, however, not all work rules are necessarily about efficiency;

many are more about enhancing the control, status, and power of managers (Ferguson 1984). The right to demand the sole attention of one or more persons, whether or not essential to completing the work, is one of the traditional rewards and symbolic enactments of power within a corporate or office setting (Kanter 1977).

In a gender (but not power) reversal of this typical scene, I was called on to play the deferential, status-enhancing role of the note taker while working as an assistant and receptionist in the president's office of a small college:

> "Kevin, why don't you grab a legal pad and a pen. Get yourself a cup of coffee if you want to and come in so we can catch up and strategize about what needs to be done," Shirley says to me as she passes my desk.
>
> "Okay," I say grabbing a pad and pen. This is not really my style, but it is steady work for the next few weeks and I can use the money. Unfortunately, I'm already wishing that it was over.
>
> "Now, what needs to be done for the board meeting next week?" Shirley begins rhetorically. "Dr. P wants it to look Christmas-y, so I've brought in a tablecloth and a few decorations already. On the day of the meeting we can move some of the poinsettias in on the table as centerpieces."
>
> "Okay." It appears that my role is more to be a sounding board and note taker.

Regardless of my other assigned tasks or duties, I was expected to drop everything and attend to Shirley's needs. Management, after all, reserves the right to dictate how and where temporaries spend their time. Symbolically, the temporary, attending to the beck and call of the supervisor, enhances the supervisor's status. Temporaries, ironically, are often under the supervision of a person quite low in the organizational hierarchy (such as a full-time secretary). Thus, they may be overcontrolled by persons with little power seeking to enhance their own status.

The de rigueur nature of adopting an appropriate demeanor became especially visible when relatively minor infractions resulted in negative social sanctions. I met negative sanctions, for example, when I refused to adopt a deferential pose on the assignment mentioned above. Shirley, the assistant to the president and my immediate supervisor, continually asserted and augmented her limited status and power through managing and controlling my time and actions while on the job (Schwartz 1973; Henley 1977). Although I always completed the assigned formal work tasks to the best of my ability, I consciously and deliberately denied Shirley the personal deference she sought.

Near the end of the my first week I arrived in the morning to find a typed message from Shirley on my chair. The note, I felt, clearly asserted the hierarchy of power and demanded my submission:

> Kevin. RE: Lunch today (12/5). My plans are to be out of the office from about 11:45 A.M. to 1:00 P.M. (If you get hungry early, I suggest you have a snack before I leave at 11:45 A.M.) Thanks. Shirl.

> This annoys me: patronizing and hostile—at least that's the way I take it. So, very casually and fully aware of the politics, I walk to Shirley's door with the note in hand and say, "Oh, about lunch . . . that's great! That works out fine with my plans too. No problem." I'm upbeat and polite, but I'm framing it as giving permission or at least as an interaction between equals.

At the end of the day I grabbed my coat, said goodnight to Shirley, and left with every intention of returning in the morning. That evening around eight o'clock, however, I received a telephone call from my agency:

> "Hi, Kevin. This is Wendy from Right. I don't know how to tell you this, but the college called us today and

they said they just didn't think things were working out.
They don't want you to come back tomorrow."
   I was stunned. "Oh."
   "Kevin, don't worry about it. It's not your problem.
She called around four-thirty and said things weren't
working out and asked if there was anyone else we could
send. We told her you were one of our best and that we
couldn't help her."

Should I have been surprised? Probably not. I was fully aware that I was
not properly playing the part. Although I had completed the formal
work adequately, I had consciously resisted adopting the appropriate
submissive demeanor. By refusing to perform the informal components
of my temporary role, I had violated role expectations. My performance
had faltered, and, as with the actor who "goes up" on his or her lines too
often, the curtain had fallen.

   For temporaries, emotional labor and impression management are
part of the job. Natalie noted the variety of acts or nuances necessary to
perform the temporary role successfully: "Temping gives you certain
coping skills in how to deal with the powers that be. You adopt a certain
persona, a way of behaving that you quickly learn. And if you don't, you
won't be temping too long. It gives you the mask to wear. It shows you
what mask to wear."

Looking Busy

   Temporary workers were expected to appear busy, demonstrating personal diligence and a strong work ethic. The organization of
the work on routine assignments compelled temporaries to be busy or be
reprimanded, but temporaries (particularly on coverage assignments),
even when they were willing and eager to perform work, were often faced
with idle time while on the job. Although temporaries on routine assignments occasionally adopted "look busy" strategies when not working (in
order to stretch the work out in a deliberate slowdown, or to steal a

private moment or an opportunity to interact with another worker), looking busy was primarily a problem for the temporary in a coverage assignment.

Rather than welcoming the lack of work, many of these temporaries said they dreaded "look busy" assignments because they dragged, seeming excruciatingly long. Olivia, for example, commented: 'I feel uncomfortable if I don't have anything to do. For one thing, it makes the time go very long. And the other thing too is that I'm being paid to do something, not to just take up space. So I prefer to be busy." Bobby Jean had a similar complaint: "I had a couple of assignments, like when I was doing reception down here, there was nothing to do. You could count how many times the phone rang. Really. It was almost a useless position." Temporary workers sometimes evaluated these coverage positions as wasteful or nonproductive ("Why didn't he just answer his own phone?" was one remark). Yet any successful business must answer its telephone calls promptly, greet its guests or clients, and be able to meet emergencies. Temporaries, in organizations as in the economy generally, may fulfill the role of reserve labor—being on hand just in case the phones get busy or a rush business memo needs to be word processed.

Some client companies, recognizing the value of just-in-case coverage work to their organizations, allow temporaries limited control over their idle time. Lillian, for example, was allowed to read on her temporary assignment at a law firm as long as she was at her desk and available to work when requested: "At the law firm I can read. I sit at my desk and read the newspaper. Really dreadful books. But they don't care if I do that. But it makes the day go by so slowly. I feel like I'm not . . . obviously, I'm not utilizing my skills at all." Jon learned that he could read, write letters, or otherwise fill his unused time on some temporary assignments:

> The funny thing is every time I've been to Kracht and
> Company I've done nothing all day long. I've answered
> three, four phone calls maybe. Taken five or six messages. And I play Tetris and Solitaire on the Macintosh.
> But they love me. And the first time I went over there to
> do Macintosh, I played games all day. Because another

temp had said. "Yeah, it's fine. And I do it all the time."
So I figured when in Rome, do as the Romans do. The
woman at the end of the day says, "Thanks for all of
your help." I had typed, like, one document for her.
Done, like, five minutes' worth. And I said, "Well, you
know, I felt really guilty playing games all day." I figured,
why should I lie to her? It's not like she didn't walk by
my desk a hundred times and see me playing. And she
was like, "No, no, no. That's our problem. If we don't
have work for you, you should do what you want." And
they called my agency and gave me a glowing review.

Whether or not any particular client company is willing to cede control over temporaries' idle time is rarely readily apparent. Connie, for
example, was explicitly told that personal business was forbidden on one
of her temporary assignments:

Oh, one time I did have a co-worker from my agency.
She was doing one assignment and I was doing another.
My supervisor that I was reporting to had seen her writing out checks, like bills. And she said, "I know you
would never do this, but I want to tell you that if I ever
catch you doing it, you're out of here. I mean personal
stuff." My supervisor said, "I expect the utmost professional behavior from you. I know you won't do it. I'm
just telling you not to do it."

Kara, though not explicitly informed, sometimes felt that using idle time
on the job for personal business was unacceptable:

Nobody ever got angry with me. But I could feel sometimes that it wasn't cool to do. I would bring things. I always had, like, a play or I'd always have, like, something
to do. Something to write, something to type. Nobody
ever outright said, "Don't do that." But there were al-

ways some places where you felt like you shouldn't do it. Everybody around you was working so hard. And granted, you really don't have anything to do but answer the phone. I would find busy work. You know, because I would feel guilty because everybody was working so hard.

Temporary workers, as in the case of physical appearance, must observe and conform to the implicit behavioral norms of each specific work setting. Often what passes for a serious normative error in one workplace is entirely acceptable in another.

Some temporaries with a well-internalized work ethic responded to their inadequate supply of tasks by making work or imposing busy work on themselves. Carol said that she found work to do during idle time on her temporary assignments:

> I did other things. You know, basically whatever . . . a lot of little things, like a lot of typing. Lots of little clerical jobs like typing labels, setting up files, things like that to keep busy. But that kind of always amazes me a little bit. Here you're paying me *x* amount of dollars and yet you're not using the skills. You could have used someone who only knows how to type. But if they're willing to pay, I'm willing to work.

Connie also created work, or worklike routines, to fill her time:

> When I was basically manning phones for a company, I mean, what are you supposed to do? I mean, you're sitting at a desk waiting for the phone to ring so you can answer it. Those were the only times there was a lull. When you had those receptionist-type assignments. And I would, like, shuffle paper. Clear up the desktop or rearrange it or go look at the files. Anything. It reminded me of McDonald's. When I used to work at McDonald's,

they, like, watched you. You could never, ever not look busy. You knew you had to scrub anything.

"If you've got time to lean, you've got time to clean," the McDonald's motto of expected work effort, may also apply to temporary work. Client companies sometimes believe that a temporary with visibly unoccupied time is being negligent in his or her duties. Inactivity is interpreted as a sign of laziness, a bad attitude, or unprofessional behavior rather than as evidence of underutilization and inefficient management of the temporaries' time.

Some temporaries responded to idle time while on assignment by requesting additional work from their client company supervisors or from nearby full-time workers. This strategy, however, frequently resulted in additional work tasks that temporaries described variously as "make work," "busy work," or "gofer work." Conscientious temps were often "rewarded" for their diligence with the least appealing, most menial dirty work of the organization. Patsy said:

> I've learned at Heyman that if you ask someone for a job, they give you, like, a career. They give you a thing that's been in their closet for six months, that's covered with dust, that's a complete mess. Nobody gives you a letter to type. It's, like, a big deal. So I just thought I'm not going to ask anybody. I mean, I'm here. I'm answering the phone.

Pamela described a "project" she was given when she requested additional work on a receptionist position:

> They said, "Go through these files and look at the dates on all these documents and if it's before 1980 throw it out." And I said, "These files?" And I was pointing at a drawer. And they said, "No. These files." And it was like a wall. "You want me to go through all these files? Okay." I'm not going to be very exact. By the time I hit

that last drawer, I have this feeling I'm going to go
"Thppt" and just throw it away.

Backlogged filing, supply-cabinet organizing, envelope stuffing, date
stamping, and other menial yet time-consuming tasks were frequently
"dumped" on temporaries who requested additional work.

Sometimes temporaries who neither requested nor created additional
work in order to make themselves look busy were assigned "dirty work" if
they appeared idle while on the job. On one of my early temporary
assignments as a receptionist (with no other assigned tasks), for example,
I was chastised for not looking busy and then used as a human staple
remover:

> "Look, I need to talk to you," Diann begins out of the
> blue, pulling up a chair to the front desk where the main
> switchboard is located. "We pay a lot of money to have
> someone here, almost as much as we get for working
> here full-time. I know you don't get much of that, but we
> pay a lot and we expect you to work and we've noticed
> that you're not working very hard. So either you work, or
> we can just forget it, okay?" she says.
>
> "Well, I told you I'm willing to work. What is it you'd
> like me to do?" I ask. Although what I really want to do
> is tell her off and march. But I am financially strapped to
> the desk.
>
> Diann shows me seven file cabinets that need to be
> "straightened up." She instructs me to "put them in re-
> verse chronological order. See how these have been sta-
> pled so many times? I want you to take out all these
> staples and restaple it once neatly in the top lefthand
> corner. And see how this date has been written in? I want
> you to use this date stamp and inkpad and stamp that
> date on in red so it's neater and easier to read."
>
> Can there be anything more pointless? Is this the rock
> farm of clerical work? I realize that Diann is spending

more time looking for "work" for me than "working"
herself.

Ironically, the imperative to look busy sometimes took precedence over
performing the formally assigned work tasks. Client company supervisors, in self-defeating rituals, would assign "dirty work" that physically
removed temporaries from the desk or phones they were specifically
hired to cover.
  Not surprisingly, temporaries who wanted to avoid "dirty work"
quickly learned not to ask for additional tasks. Some, like Bobby Jean,
forged ahead, claiming control over their idle time unless told otherwise:
"I read a book all day. I was, like, 'I'm sorry, but unless you have envelopes for me to stuff, I'm reading my book and my newspaper.' And it
seemed to be okay. No one yelled at me or anything." This strategy,
however, may invite formal sanction, particularly if the temporaries appear to be relaxing or enjoying themselves. Like an actor on the stage,
temps must remain in character, observing the action and responding
appropriately.
  Temporaries developed a number of strategies to deal with this di-
lemma—how to look busy and productive when there is no "real" work.
They soon learned to bring personal (yet unobtrusive) things to do with
them on assignment, what one temp described as her "boredom bag."

> I've got books. I've got stationery and envelopes, maga-
> zines, bills to pay, my bank statement. Balance my check-
> book. A calculator, because many of them don't have
> calculators. I forget what my first assignment was, but I
> went out at lunch time and bought a magazine because I
> couldn't handle not having anything to do. (Kimberly)

Steve, an actor, described a similar, if occupation-specific, assortment: "I
always brought books, always brought my own work. I had a mailing to
go out, letters that I had to write to agents or something, scripts to
memorize and work on. Always brought that stuff. Because you sit a lot.
A lot!"

Because they are located in highly visible areas, however, whatever they do, temps must be exceptionally careful not to give off (Goffman 1959) indicators that say "not busy." Bobby Jean, for example, commented: "I always had time to do personal work. In fact, a lot of times when I was trying to look busy I did that. Write letters to friends and stuff like that. Because it does make you look busy and they don't know what you're doing. If you can get away with it. Usually, I could." Temporary workers occupy an awkward position of being socially invisible yet very physically visible in the office (see Rogers 1995). Full-time workers entrenched in the personal networks of the office and known as "good workers" may occasionally be allowed to appear idle or take a break, but temporaries are allowed little leeway; every action or nonaction is suspect. Temporaries therefore claimed control over their idle time by adopting strategies that circumvented this visibility-invisibility predicament.

Temporaries pursued personal activities that gave the impression (Goffman 1959) that they were diligently completing organizational tasks. Writing personal letters, journal entries, cover letters, résumés, short stories, homework, poetry, or, in my case, field notes at the computer was a commonly adopted strategy for looking busy: "The last long-term assignment I had, I typed two of my term papers. And that was helpful. You know, just as long as I look busy. That's part of my job, to look professional. And sitting at your desk doing your nails is not professional" (Joanne). Additionally, temporaries sometimes used tricks that assisted them in their impression management:

> I'll usually call up real work on one screen. Switch to the
> other screen to work on my stuff. The good old Word-
> Perfect switch screen. I love that. I love that. I had one
> job where, like, for a week I didn't have any work. So I
> would keep my work on a work page on a document
> that was a real document. And anytime anyone came,
> up, I'd just go to page one and there I was. (Patsy)

Temporary workers, tailoring their look-busy strategies to each setting, took account of an implicit hierarchy of discreetness. Writing, for example, was believed to be more discreet than reading; reading was believed to be more discreet than talking on the phone. Within these "leisure" activities even more subtle distinctions were made. Jon, for example, felt that reading, if not highly visible, was appropriate: "A lot of times I will ask, 'Is it all right if I read? Is it okay if I read the paper?' Because a lot of times it's better if you read a book than the paper, 'cause the paper is spread out over your desk. A book is more subtle." Bobby Jean, however, believed she needed to be physically doing something in order to appear busy:

> You kind of learn how to get away with that kind of
> stuff. But there was nothing to do. And the problem too
> was it was a place where they took a lot of money. And
> they didn't really want me handling the money, so there
> was not much they could do as far as that. But as long as
> I was physically doing something and not reading a
> book, that was better. It looked better on them.

Temporaries were required to make these fine distinctions, understanding the norms of each company and adopting the appropriate behaviors.

Some temporaries resorted to look-busy strategies that required the physical transformation of their leisure materials into officelike props. Like any graduate of public education in the United States, temporaries read at will by concealing their books, magazines, and other materials inside the covers of software manuals, dictionaries, or other office-appropriate books. Bob, using the client company photocopier, transformed his leisure reading into an official-looking document: "They really frown on reading magazines and books. So I bring my book in and go to the photocopier and, you know, photocopy the first fifty pages and pretend I'm shuffling papers and just read my book." Similarly, Patsy photocopied her "crossword out of the newspaper and then put a document on top." By converting books, crossword puzzles, or articles to 8½-by-11-inch office stock or concealing them in nonanachronistic office objects, temporaries could control their idle time without visually disrupting their performance of diligent temporary office worker. Like stage actors convincing the audience that the tinted-water, make-believe cocktails are intoxicating or the blank gun has created a mortal wound, temporary workers convince their audiences that they are assiduously performing organizational tasks with make-believe office props.

The telephone, though clearly belonging to the office setting, was a problematic prop. Successful executives are expected to spend a great deal of their work time on the phone, but secretaries, temporary or otherwise, are expected to field and route telephone calls quickly—they are a conduit or facilitator of the "important" communications of superiors rather than communicators in and of themselves. Brief calls, however, could be "pulled off" by using a serious, lower-register, "office" voice: "I call my answering machine. And you have to make it look like this is business. My friend used to do that. He'd call me from his temp job and talk, like, in a really low voice. Very serious. He would talk, 'Uh huh. Absolutely.' But you just do it discreetly" (Kara). But the temporary worker on the phone for extended periods, like the temporary reading a book or newspaper, quickly gives off "not busy" signals:

> S: That was my problem. Because I tended to be on the phone a lot. Because if I ran out of stuff to do, rather than just sit there looking stupid, I just got on the phone.
> KH: Did anyone ever give you any hassles about that?
> S: Always. Always. And I would say, "Oh, I'm terribly sorry." And do it again. It bothered me at first, a lot. But then I finally said, "Fuck it."
> KH: Did you try to make it sound like business?
> S: Oh sure, sure. But you know if you're a temp, what business you got on the phone?! If anything, I would say, "I'm calling my agency." "What for?" "I don't know."

The combination of boredom, social isolation, and access to a telephone creates a tempting atmosphere, verging on entrapment, for some temporary workers. These factors, combined with the high probability of detection, may account for the prevalence of prohibitions against personal telephone calls put forth by temporary agencies. From the temporary industry's perspective, complaints regarding their workers' "excessive" personal phone use are a routine problem. But like the Reagan and Bush administrations' "just say no" response to illicit drug use, a policy prohibiting personal phone use does not address the underlying problem.

This emphasis on how hard temporaries should work, rather than on how well they complete their assigned tasks, is also often offensive, humiliating, and stressful for temporary workers. Daniel resented looking busy so much, for example, that he would occasionally request to be sent home early:

> You tell them, "What do you want me to do? There's
> nothing to do. I'll go home." Or you just look busy. But
> I hate doing that. But basically I say, "Just send me home
> if there's nothing to do. I'm not trying to be rude." But
> I'd rather do that than try to look busy. It's very, very
> stressful to try to look busy and try to conform to this
> nebulous kind of rule—look busy.

Regardless of their willingness to work, temporary workers are suspected of laziness and untrustworthiness. Ironically, temporaries who attempt to comply with the imperative to look busy, yet who fail in their impression management efforts (such as the temp who is "caught" writing personal letters or playing computer games), confirm stereotypes of temporaries as indolent or otherwise inept workers.

As in the case of appearance, the imperative that temporaries look busy may be more for the discipline of full-time employees. Temporaries may recognize the importance of completing formal work tasks to the best of their ability, but they often miss the significance of playing their organizational part credibly:

> My part of the bargain is I go in there with the attitude
> I'm going to work, I'm going to take my time, I'm going

to do things with integrity. But the opposite part of the agreement is that you show me how to do what I need to do, you tell me who I need to go to when I have problems, you support me when I need support, and you don't ask me to do stupid things. Like things that are just so that I look busy. Because that's demeaning, I think, and it's pointless. (Aleshia)

Far from being "pointless," the mandate to look busy, regardless of the actual formal work demands, may be seen as essential to securing an adequate work effort from everyone in the office.

The struggle over appropriate levels of work effort is nothing new. Full-time staff members worry that temporaries will be "rate busters," completing more work than regular staff and raising the ante on appropriate levels of work effort (Hughes 1984). Client company supervisors, however, worry that temporaries who appear visibly idle challenge management's authority to define appropriate levels of effort. Temporaries, then, are often third parties caught between the warring factions of full-time labor and management, each attempting to control the definition of what constitutes a fair day's work. Looking busy, in other words, is the opposite of rate busting but part and parcel of the same puzzle.

Conclusion

Out of necessity temporaries soon realize that they must not only possess the skills to produce the required work but also look and play the part if they wish to continue working. Temporary workers, as part of proper job performance, are required to call on a repertoire of impression management and emotional labor techniques and invest scarce personal resources to adopt the client company's desired appearance.

These command performances may be essential to maintaining the structure of relations in the office. Temporary workers must observe the client company's rules and norms regarding appearance, demeanor, and appropriate level of work effort for the company to maintain the legitimacy of these claimed privileges or areas of control over all their employees, core or contingent. Allowing anyone, even a temporary worker, to break the rules, management fears, may erode the company's control and discipline.

Although client companies have fundamentally altered the employer-employee relationship, they have not modified their expectations. Client companies want committed workers yet resist investing resources in their contingent employees. Temporaries also resist investing their scarce resources in their short-term employers. Consequently, conflicts over appearance, demeanor, and work effort may be the localized sites of temporary worker resistance against management-imposed control.

6 *Just a Temp*

> Where I work on a long-term temporary assignment
> there's a lot of people who I graduated from college with
> on staff. And when they see me, you know, they go, "What
> are you doing? Why are you working as a temporary secre-
> tary?!" There's a lot of . . . I don't know. Maybe it's all in my
> mind because I feel sort of inferior to that because they're
> kind of established. I feel really inadequate. (Bob)

Occupation is one of the primary ways in which we iden-
tify ourselves and are identified by others. "What do you do?" is the first
thing we are likely to be asked after introductions in most adult social
settings. And most of us respond with an explanation of our paid labor
activity, giving our job title, naming our employer, or describing our
particular "bundle of tasks." As Everett Hughes noted, "A man's work is
one of the more important parts of his social identity, of his self, of his
fate, in the one life he has to live" (1984, 339).

This self-defining characteristic of work, along with the relatively low
status of their own economic activity, is not lost on temporary workers.
Nor is it lost on those with whom they interact on or off the job.

Temporaries are repeatedly confronted with the inadequacy of their occupational "choice" (they may be asked, for example, "When are you going to get a 'real' job?") and the alleged personal deficiencies their temporary employment implies. Indeed, in this sense, working as a temporary is a stigma, a stigma that carries with it negative assumptions about an individual's qualifications, abilities, and character.

When temporary workers interact with others who perceive them as temporaries, they are confronted with their deviance. Temporaries cannot simply ignore the stigma of their imputed social identity. Like other stigmatized groups, temporaries can either internalize the stigma, incorporating it into their self-concept, or adopt strategies to deny, deflect, or manage it (Goffman 1961, 1963; Scott 1969).

The Erosion of Self-Esteem

Temporaries, both on and off the job, must face the inadequacy of their occupation and the unfitness, ineptness, or undesirability their temporary employment implies. Lillian, for example, described the social embarrassment she felt when asked "What do you do?":

> The worst part about temping is probably when people ask you what you do. It's, like, "Oh, you're doing temp work still, Lillian? Can't you get a job?" That's a big one. My parents are, like, " Lillian, let's get a job." They're really, like, "Why did you go to a private liberal arts college? Why did we spend all this money for you to go to this school?"

Lillian was confronted with a status incongruity: she was college-educated yet still employed in low-status, low-wage work. Her position in the occupational structure, in the eyes of others, implied at best inadequacies or ineptitude in her job-seeking abilities and at worst that their perceptions of her had been false.

Kimberly also noted the difficulties of explaining why she was working as a temporary:

> When you meet somebody new who's your age and they
> say, "Oh, what do you do?" I kind of swallow and say,
> "I'm temping right now, but . . . " Because I think it very
> much is. . . . We're in a status society and what you do is
> very important. Talking to friends of mine that I went to
> college with about their jobs and "Oh, they've just been
> promoted to this and this. Now what are you doing?"
> "Well, I'm still temping now." "Oh. Well . . . " It's a kind
> of feeling that they're moving so far with their career and
> I'm just kind of staying temping. And yet I know that I
> don't want a career like theirs.

Although some temporaries know that they don't want a typical career
and others, given current economic conditions and the changing occupational opportunity structure, can't find a "real" job, the social legitimacy automatically accorded full-time, permanent employees (normals)
compared to temporaries' present circumstances is hard to deny to both
self and others.[1]

Similarly, their relative status in the workplace is made painfully clear
to temporaries: they are "just the temp." Temporaries, like the occupants
of other low-status roles prefaced with the qualifier "just," are identified
exclusively with (or as) their devalued occupational category.[2] As Steve
said: "Well, they assume right away that you're a moron because you're a
temp, rather than accepting that you just have something else going on."
In other words, individuals involved in temporary work are assigned the
deviant "master status" of temporary regardless of other possible social
statuses they could take on (Hughes 1945; Becker 1963). Besides this
conflation of the individual with the organizational category ("just the
temp"), assumptions are made about workers' qualifications, abilities,
and character generally ("just a temp"). These assumptions of deviance
are expressed through face-to-face interactions, the organization of the
work, and the physical layout of the workplace.

One marker of the extent to which "temporary worker" becomes an
individual's master status in the workplace is the depersonalizing manner
in which "co-workers" frequently fail to learn or use a temporary's name:

"But you'd go to these places and people are always like, 'Temp. Temp. There's a temp.' And you'd get that, 'The temp.' You'd have a couple nice people, but for the most part in a big office people go, 'Where's the temp? What's the temp doing?' You know, you never had a name" (Pamela). Failing to learn someone's name, in many contexts, is a sign of disrespect or an indicator of unequal status. The successful completion of the temporary assignment requires temporaries to learn the permanent workers' names and faces, primarily for the performance of communication tasks, but "co-workers" often do not feel compelled, even out of courtesy, to learn and use the temporary's name. Although that may simply be an outgrowth of the relatively short duration of the temporary's tenure, temporary workers are denied their individuality as unique, interesting, and worthwhile persons when treated categorically as "just the temp."

In interactions with supervisors and co-workers, assumptions are made and communicated to temps about their ability (or inability) to handle even low-skill tasks. Bob, for example, found requests to set work aside "until so-and-so gets back" condescending: "People assume that you're just a temp. There's, like, this whole 'just a temp' attitude among the permanent employees. And it's kind of like 'Don't give him this because he probably won't know how to do it.' It's just really insulting." Similarly, Susan complained that she was treated "like a moron" by her co-workers on a temporary assignment:

> When I started temping at the real estate development
> corporation, I was sitting there and one of the guys came
> out and he said, "Here, would you make copies of this?"
> Tracy, a permanent secretary, goes, "Oh, here. I'll do
> that." Like I'm going to screw it up, you know? So every
> time someone came up, Tracy would go, "Here. I'll do
> that. I'll do that." So I sat there and I said, "Knock your
> socks off, bitch. If you want to run your legs off, you go
> right ahead. I'll sit here and make my *x* number of dol-
> lars per hour. If you want to do all the work, go ahead. I
> don't mind a bit." She did not think I was capable of

> doing the work they were giving me. But they do treat
> you like you're a moron, and that's the hard part.

Temporaries find themselves patronized and demeaned in a variety of ways, besides being asked to put aside work they know is well within their capabilities. Simple tasks are overexplained, intensely supervised, and effusively complimented when completed. I was particularly irritated by overdone praises for my work. On several occasions I was complimented on my typing speed, told that I did a "nice job on the memo," and left perky thank-you notes ("Mornin', Kevin—I've gone through all of our information. You're doing *a super job!* Thanks!"). These work episodes remind temporary workers of the low opinions others generally hold of temporaries and their work abilities.

The relatively low value of a temporary's time is evident in both their low wages and the way their time is controlled and used by others in the workplace. For example, temporaries not only often take their lunch alone; they also take it at everyone else's convenience (including permanent employees nominally at the same level):

> They felt free to be more abusive. You know, like you
> weren't human. "No, you can't go to eat lunch until so-
> and-so goes to lunch. You have to cover the phones while
> they're gone." So sometimes you end up eating . . . like,
> your lunch time was always weird compared to every-
> body else's. You were always the last. (Pamela)

Additionally, temporaries are, as part of their work, expected to screen callers (protecting the "valuable" time of permanent people in the organization) and generally do the bulk of time-consuming, low-status, and routine work, such as photocopying, opening mail, filing, fetching coffee, greeting guests, and office "housekeeping."

Exclusion from regular sociability routines, although usually done without malice, further reinforces the temporary's "otherness" and low standing in the workplace. Temporaries, for example, are rarely included when permanent employees break their work routine for a shared cup of coffee or a trip to the vending machine. Temporaries are also commonly left out of office birthday, holiday, retirement, and other celebrations. A temporary may in fact be used to facilitate office sociability by providing phone or other work coverage for permanent employees on these occasions. One temporary described an assignment in which her sole duty was to cover—with a less than truthful story—for the permanent office staff members while they enjoyed their holiday party.

Even the relative size, comfort, and privacy of their work settings and furnishings impress on temporaries that they are at the bottom of the corporate hierarchy. At one of my temporary assignments in a large Chicago law firm, for example, the clerical furniture (huddled in a common, public, windowless island toward the interior of the building) consisted of half-back, low chairs without arms, whereas the attorneys (in their private offices with expansive views of the city) had deep, reclining leather chairs with arms. Furthermore, the limited work space and layout of desks, typing tables, and computer stations enforced a position of holding in one's body, keeping the knees together, and generally taking up very little space. These setting-induced positions are powerless ("feminine") body postures (Henley 1977) and act as one more symbolic reminder to temporaries, and clerical workers in general, of their subordinate status within the corporation.

These continual verbal and nonverbal assaults on one's self-concept[3] become increasingly difficult for temporaries to escape, deny, or deflect. Over time many temporaries begin to experience a loss of self-confidence, a painful erosion of self-esteem, as these unflattering views are (at least partially) internalized. Pamela, for example, commented:

> It was hard. It wasn't hard the way I thought it was going to be hard. I thought it was going to be hard because they were going to ask me to do some office thing that I didn't know how to do, till I found out that usually office things don't take that long to do. Although they usually think it takes a long time. But it was hard emotionally.

Emotionally hard. It sounds so dramatic, but it was to me. It was really a drag. At the time I was a weeping, crying fool in parking lots all over. A lot of jobs. The way they treated me, I just felt like, "Lighten up, man. Be nice to me." People work a lot better when you're nice to them. So in that respect, I didn't expect it to be such a traumatic thing. Because by the time I was done I was like . . . it took a while to bolster that self-confidence.

Helen described how the work assaulted her self-concept and how her lack of embeddedness and the way in which others evaluated, regarded, or failed to regard her were occasionally too much to bear:

One morning I was walking to the train to go to my temporary job and I started to cry! You know, nobody gives a shit about you! You could drop dead and they wouldn't notice. They'd just get another temp. It's a little overdramatic, of course. You just feel like you're very wrapped up in this futile routine. And it's just too much. It's really upsetting. I've really dreaded going in some days.

Temporaries, confronted with assumptions about who they are and how they ought to behave, are forced to respond in some manner.[4]

Passing as Normal

So that they may survive emotionally and protect their self-concept, temporaries devise ways of buttressing their sense of self from the stigma and assaults of temporary work. Particularly at the beginning of their tenure, temporaries may pursue a strategy of blurring the lines or boundaries of their temporary role in an attempt to "pass" as normals (Goffman 1963). In this strategy temporaries assimilate themselves into the organization and say, "I belong here. I am more and can do more than be just a temporary for you." Joanne, for example, described her strategy for fitting in on temporary assignments:

It just takes five or ten minutes to give me the basics. And that's what I like about it too. It's very challenging mentally to go into a place, to set up a rapport with people you've never seen before and you may never see again in life. And to instantly, just about, pick up what needs they have. Incorporate what knowledge you have of how businesses run. Put it all together and have the place operating fairly smoothly. My goal is so that people don't even know that there's a temp there. I want to be invisible to the point that I don't want a lot of mistakes and that, where people say, "Oh. That temp!" You know, that kind of negative thing. I want to portray myself in such a way that I'm here to help. I'm helping. And I'm a plus to your company and not a minus. And that's my personal goal.

Temporary workers who can fit in with the team, make themselves seem indispensable, and gain the respect of their co-workers conceal the stigma of their temporary status.

Seeking Continuity

Seeking placement in a known industry such as insurance, banking, or accounting allows temporaries to draw on previous work experiences to conceal the temporary status of their current employment and pass for normals or permanent employees of the organization. A comfortable setting with a familiar work lingo, as Ginny noted, can be an effective resource for a credible performance as a permanent employee:

At AdvertLand it was wonderful, because I do know something about commercial production. I do know something about TV production and ads and copyrighting and everything. And I was able to make sense to these clients that would call in. And I knew what I was talking about. And it was wonderful. I would hate to be sent to, like, an accounting firm or a real estate firm or something like that. Because it would be, like, "What the hell is going on?"

Although the content of the work may be very different, at least the setting and lingo are congruent with a previous or preferred self.[5]

Doing "Quality Work" and Bumping up the Skill

Temporaries can blur the lines of their temporary role by becoming a "super" employee. Through acting in the capacity of a computer consultant, computer trainer, or graphic designer, one can be more than just a temporary to both self and co-workers. Bobby Jean described how she took on extra tasks, framing herself more as a consultant than a temporary, on one of her assignments:

> I ended up automating their office. Because they were taking preprinted letters and trying to line them up on the typewriter to try to get the name and address right. And I'm looking at this like, "This is stupid." This is the computer age. And you have a computer sitting over there that can do this. And so I put, like, the letters . . . and I did it really easy for them. I didn't even do a merge. I just did "date" and "address." I said, "Just delete this. Type over it. Print it. And don't save it. Or save it under another name. But just leave your blank. And you can pull this up whenever you want it."

Pamela recounted how she adopted the role of computer trainer and teacher on an assignment:

> They had just bought computers for everybody. Nobody had had a computer before 1988. And all of a sudden the company said everyone must have a computer. And then I walked in and I knew all these different software packages. People were just popping software packages onto their machines. So even though I was there specifically to send out a form letter . . . that's why I was really

there, because I knew how to do mail merge on Display-
write 4. But as it turned out, I did that really quickly.
And I started to support all these secretaries on their PC
packages. So they kept me because I was helping everybody. Actually, I did a class for these guys. And pretty
soon everybody . . . like, the head of sales administration
was like, "Who is that person?"

Through taking the role of a nonstigmatized but nonpermanent office
worker, temporaries attempted to obscure the temporary status of their
organizational role and pass as normal. By doing quality work or bump-
ing up the skill level, temporaries, in effect, say, "I'm more than just a
temporary—I'm a valuable player on your team."[6]

Saving the Bosses

Temporaries may also blur the lines of their organizational
role or status by engaging in a tactic of saving the bosses from their own
errors. As Everett C. Hughes noted, a "common dignifying rationalization of people in all positions of a work hierarchy except the very top one
is, 'We in this position save the people in the next higher position above
from their own mistakes'" (Hughes 1984, 340–41). Aleshia, for example, attempted to keep her boss from overexplaining:

She basically wrote what basically could have been a
merge letter with three variations. And instead of saying,
"Here's a list of people. Everyone gets this information.
That's stock. He gets inset A and B. He gets insert C,"
she wrote out every letter. And instead of just saying basically what I just said, "You'll notice that each letter is a
little bit different. Make sure that you follow my letter,"
she said, "Now this letter has something different." She
sat down and explained every letter. After about seven
letters, I said, "Delia, I think I've got it." And I have a lot
of work to do. I don't have time for bullshit like that. I
don't get offended, because I know I'm intelligent and I
don't need to prove that to her. How could a woman

with this little logic, it's a basic logic function, pairing
functions, saying the basic plus the variant. She doesn't
have a grasp of that. Why is this woman in a management position? Well, maybe she has some other qualities
that . . . this isn't one of them.

Similarly, Mary attempted to correct grammatical errors in her bosses'
work:

> Because I studied English I'll edit their, the bosses', work
> a lot and they'll notice that and they don't like it. It's an
> insult to them that someone would be doing this. And
> I'll say, "But I teach English. That's what I normally do."
> Which even bothers them more, I think. That they have
> an educated secretary on their hands. You know, a lot of
> these men are kind of insecure. But no, the men, they
> don't like their work to be edited. I think they just want
> someone to sit down and do the work.

While catching mistakes may improve one's own status within the organization, it can also be fraught with tension in actual usage. Operating
on one-upmanship—publicly pointing out the ignorance or errors of
those higher in the hierarchy—may not be a particularly endearing tech-
nique for passing as normal. Temporaries who can "help" their bosses
correct errors without offending or publicly challenging the hierarchy
(that is, framing corrections in a less assertive or confrontational style
such as a suggestion, a question, or a comment with a tag question—
"*Commitment* is spelled with two *m*'s, isn't it?"),[7] may more successfully
blur the boundaries of the temporary role.

Securing Long-Term Assignments

One of the most effective ways to obscure the boundaries of
one's temporary role and pass as a normal is to secure long-term assignments. An extended stay of several weeks or months within a single client
company (or return assignments) routinizes the presence of the temporary in the workplace to the point that he or she may be mistaken for a

permanent employee. Susan, for example, noted that the difficulties of managing assumptions about self were reduced in long-term assignments: "It is truly tough to go to a new company and prove yourself. I was so glad that I was able to stay at the real estate development corporation and the law firm, because they knew that I wasn't a dummy." Daniel, also noted the way in which longer-term assignments allowed one to "break through" (Davis 1961) the assumed stigma(s):

> When I walk into an office and they see me, they have certain expectations right away. I open my mouth, and I speak in a certain way, and they don't know how to handle it. Being treated as a black male, and then having a certain amount of intelligence, they don't know how to deal with you. If you're there for a week, that's fine. If you're there for a month, then they eventually get to know Daniel and I eventually get to know them. So it's that kind of thing.

Long-term assignments, then, allow individuation and differentiation from the category of just a temp. Temporaries in these assignments can reveal enough other social information eventually to break through and disavow their deviant identity.[8] Whereas permanent workers may say that they've been someplace so long they're beginning to feel like part of the furniture, temporaries who stay on the same assignment say they begin to feel less like a piece of furniture and more like a person.

Telling the Cover Story

One of the most common strategies for managing the stigma of working as a temporary is to invoke the "cover story." The cover story, which is told to both self and others, presents an alternative identity and explains and legitimates one's presence in an otherwise stigmatizing situation.[9] Through bringing in one's supporting props (providing additional social information) and reinterpreting and rationalizing narrative-disrupting or discordant elements, temporaries attempt to build a supporting and believing audience for their alternative identity performance. In short, temporaries, through the cover story, claim an alternative "master status" or basis for their identity—"Well, I'm working as a temporary, but I'm not really a temporary. I'm really this."

Verbally telling one's cover story to co-workers, providing social information about self not readily available in the workplace, was one common strategy temporaries employed in the effort to disavow or cover their stigma. Bob, for example, noted how temporaries without prompting would share their cover stories, revealing their "underlying reason" for presence in a stigmatic situation:

> I don't want to say that they're not proud of being temps, but they want you to know that there is another reason that they are temping. I mean, you don't have to ask, "So what's your story?" Well, "before I get a real job" or "in between shows." There's always that little subtlety. Even secretaries too, but not as much as temps, sort of let you know that there is a reason why they're doing this and that it's not a copout. An underlying reason. A more worthwhile underlying reason.

Steve, who used this strategy, told me that he always informed his co-workers that he was an actor:

> S: Oh, I always told them I was an actor. Immediately. Immediately. And they were, like, "Great! This is wonderful." So maybe that's what cut the ice, you know. They knew I wasn't just waiting to get a "real job." "Why doesn't this guy have a real job yet?"
> KH: So you told them right away?
> S: Sure. I'm a temp. This is what I do. This is what I want to do because I'm an actor.

Through the telling of their personal circumstances and the articulation of their cover story for temping, temporary workers attempted to differentiate and distance themselves from the stigma of temporary work.[10]

The opportunity to tell the cover story, however, does not always arise easily and naturally for temporaries. Consequently, some temporaries openly wished that their agencies would intervene to facilitate the individuation process, providing personalized introductions or placements in settings where the work would spontaneously allow revelations of more positive social information:

> I'm fluent in German. And I have all these artistic skills. And I know a little bit of Moroccan Arabic and some French. And I go, like, "God. Why can't I temp in a German bank?" Or something like that. That would be really neat. These things are never even mentioned. The agency could mention to the person where you're being placed on assignment that you were in the Peace Corps or that you have an education. None of that seems to be conveyed at all. (Helen)

The extent to which temporaries desire and consciously seek opportunities to tell their cover story was revealed in an anecdote I was told by a temporary counselor:

> I had a temporary once. Her name was Laura. And she was an executive secretary, and she had very good skills. I think she had low self-esteem from being a temporary. And she told me once, "Cindy, what I think I'm going to do is type up a letter about myself and just hand it to people. And say I'm Laura Naiman, I am not just a temporary and da, da, da, da, da." I was, "Laura, no." She was so caught up, she was so embarrassed that she was a temporary. (Cindy)

Using Supporting Props

One way of creating appropriate openings in which to tell the cover story is to conspicuously carry alternative identity props or "prestige symbols" (Goffman 1963). Some temporaries are never seen without a "self"-revealing book; others wear lapel pins or carry their business cards, résumés, theatrical scripts, backpacks, or textbooks in support of an alternative self.

> Sometimes they ask, "What are you doing?" Or I'll be reading a book on Windsor Castle. "Oh, what's that?" You know, that kind of thing. And I'll say, "Well . . . " I'm always eager to talk about my documentary project on Windsor Castle. You know, if you talk about it, it may happen. Sometimes I need that little opportunity to say, "Yes, I am really working for that. And not for six dollars and twenty five cents." (Daniel)

A carefully chosen prop will often give the desired impression (Goffman 1959) or elicit questions creating an appropriate context in which to tell the cover story and reveal positive social information about one's self.

On one occasion when I found myself working near another temporary, I initiated a conversation (hoping to request a formal interview) by asking about her book bag, which bore the logo of a well-known Chicago theater company. She cheerfully told me that she interned at the theater and was currently looking for steady technical theater work. Over the course of the week that we worked together, I heard her repeat her story, almost verbatim, to several others who inquired about her ubiquitous book bag. Similarly, I relied heavily on my cover story: "I'm a graduate student." I carried my backpack and chose scholarly books as prestige symbols. Indeed, although I was teaching an introductory sociology course one night a week, I did not want to be seen with the textbook: it did not signify the desired prestige (I did not want to be mistaken for an undergraduate student).

Even when props do not directly elicit the opportunity to tell the cover story to others, they can be used to buttress one's chosen identity in a performance for the self.[11] Like carefully chosen stage props, temporaries' props supported the enactment of their chosen character.

> I had a lapel pin at one of my really lax jobs. It says in Arabic, "We Are All One People." And it has a little pic-

ture of a globe. And people would notice that and I
would tell them. So that was kind of cool. Sometimes I
have my Morocco pictures and I look at them while I'm
at lunch or something. Or I have it like a pile. You desperately want to preserve that connection. Like, yes, I do
have a life outside of this. This is temporary, but . . .
(Helen)

Reinterpreting and Rationalizing

Even elements of the work situation that at first appear
constraining to the development or expression of an alternative self are
creatively interpreted by temporaries as resources. I believed, for example, that temporaries, required to play the part of an office worker, were
denied the opportunity for self-expression and characterization through
costume. One temporary I interviewed, however, had reinterpreted her
"corporate" or "temporary" look as consistent with her acting career:

> KH: Did you have to buy special clothes when you
> started temping?
> L: Yes! Only because I had no clothes. I didn't have
> any suits. That was another thing. When I started temp-
> ing and started applying for jobs and stuff, I had to get a
> suit. But I also had to get a suit for industrial acting au-
> ditions too. So what I would use for my industrial
> look . . . you know, at the same time because of the cor-
> porate look and things like that. Because my style of
> dress is not like that.

Others reinterpreted experiences on the job as being useful for other life
projects: emotional material to draw on for stage portrayals, talents for
dealing with others, or skills and experiences that could be helpful in
selling oneself on the "real" job market. What might at first appear as
frivolous hairsplitting is actually identity work, work that is useful to
temporaries in closing the gap between a preferred identity and an assigned identity.

Some temporaries even reinterpreted their lowly position within the corporate hierarchy as a virtue: their low status is the admirable result of their rejection of injurious mainstream values and conceptions of success. If they wanted to play corporate America's game, they could win at it, but they are not interested:

> When you see the seamy sides of what you're doing, that's just really awful. Working for a company that developed regional shopping malls, I became alerted to articles about malls. I couldn't stop myself. They banned protesters against the Gulf War from demonstrating in the mall. "It's not a public place." They don't even let the Salvation Army in there. I guess you can see their point if you're a ruthless capitalist. There's just some sort of seedy things. I just hate that whole hierarchy. It's just so awful. I mean, the secretaries are mistreated. The politics are hideous. There's so much backstabbing. You don't approve of what they're doing in the first place. I guess I'm not even interested in being in the corporate arena at all. I don't want any of it. I hate all of it together. It's just feeling very alienated. Hope it's over soon. (Helen)

By claiming to want no part of it at all, whether truthful or just sour grapes, temporaries can deflect the stigma of occupying one of the corporate sector's low-ranking positions.

Building a Supportive Audience

It doesn't matter terribly whether the cover story is "true" or not. It does matter, however, whether you can get others to believe and help support it. Plenty of people who call themselves actors, for example, rarely (or never) appear in a dramatic production. Telling the cover story to co-workers is one way of enlisting others in constructing an alternative conception of self—if others believe it, it may just come true.[12]

> The people who I worked with were really sweet. They were infatuated with the fact that I was an actor, but they

really couldn't understand it. So I was, like, in this situation where I was kind of my own entity among all these people. You know, it was real hard to fit in anywhere. 'Cause it wasn't something that I would do as a career choice. (Sergei)

Audiences, on or off the job, that accept the enactment of alternative or "normal" selves are helpful to temporaries in denying their deviance, recuperating from the stresses of demeaning treatment on the job, and bolstering their preferred identity or self-concept.

The temporary who successfully asserts his or her cover story breaks through many of the stigmatizing assumptions associated with being "just a temp." Many temporaries, like Helen, reported that they went from being treated categorically and stereotypically as "just a temp" to being treated individually and given more respect when they divulged their cover story:

Some places they ask you, "Oh, are you in school?" I guess because I'm relatively young or whatever. And I tell them I just was in the Peace Corps. And then, oh my God! It's like the floodgates open. And suddenly you were on an equal footing. And this other man brought in all these articles about Madagascar for me, because I said I might be going there. Yeah, and suddenly you were treated much differently. But as soon as they find out that you've had any education, or whatever, they really change.

Natalie also noted the change in interaction with others when social information was revealed and acknowledged:

I think most people know that I've just finished this graduate program. And so I think . . . and if they didn't know . . . what I do notice is that when someone didn't know and they find out, there's a behavioral change toward me. Like all of a sudden, "Oh!" And there's a certain amount of respect accorded me that might have just . . . not that it wasn't accorded to me before, it just wasn't there. Like there's a certain amount of attention given to me as an individual when certain facts about my background come out.

"Suddenly, you were on an equal footing" and "There's a certain amount of attention given to me as an individual" are expressions of breaking through initial categorical and stereotypical treatment to recognition as an individual with a name, a personal history, and worth.

Constructing the Self in Opposition to Others

When asserting definitional control over one's identity through the strategies of passing as normal and telling the cover story is unsuccessful, temporaries may paradoxically attempt to maintain their alternative identity through a tactic of silence, avoidance, and stigmatization of others. By not revealing their alternative identity, by withholding the cover story, temporaries can preserve and nurture their preferred self both privately and in the company of known, safe audiences. Kirk, for example, pursued a strategy of protecting and controlling his social information: "Yeah, I pretty much prefer not talking too much or revealing much about myself at all at these places. I think it could be a pretty demeaning experience in lots of ways except that I think that you and I and people like us can really shrug off people saying things to us that might sort of insult our intelligence." Similarly, Pamela described attempts to maintain control over her personal information:

> There were the people who were like, "You have a degree. Why don't you get a job. What are you, a goof?" I'm like, "No, I'm not a goof. I want to write. I want to write in advertising, but there aren't any jobs." But, yeah, a lot of people were really curious why I was temping. I think I usually said I was interviewing and looking for full-time work. A lot of the times when they were asking me, it was

the people who were, you know, "the temp" kind of people who were, "Why don't you . . . ?" And I really didn't want to answer their questions. You know what I mean? Because it wasn't like they were really interested in why you were a temp. They were more like, "Uh . . . [distaste sound]." Like that. It's because, like, "I'm broke."

Maintaining control over one's personal information maintained social distance from normals in the workplace. For temporaries to acknowledge that these others were worth talking to was also to acknowledge that their positive judgments were desired and sought.

Additionally, telling one's dreams and aspirations puts them out on the line for public inspection and exposes them to judgments, judgments that may be less than kind. Daniel, for example, sometimes attempted to protect his dream through a strategy of information control:

> If somebody asks, I tell them that I'm an independent film director. But I try not to because . . . you know, then you have to go back, it's a dream, but it's also a dream that I'm working on. But still it reinforces the fact that I'm working nine to five, whatever job it is that I need to work. So a lot of things come up other than my life as a closet movie director or producer. But I usually don't bring it up, because I just found that it's depressing at times.

Even simple questions ("Oh, you're an actor. What have you been in?"), asked in innocence, may challenge and threaten one's alternative conception of self. Experiences that are less than fully affirming, over time with many placements, may make one less willing to divulge personal information on the job.

At Least I'm Not a Secretary

Interactions with other temporary or permanent secretaries may also be avoided to minimize the stigma of association and the ever-present, ever-threatening fear that one might really belong.[13] Natalie, for example, described how she avoided associating, at least at first, with permanent secretaries:

> When I first was starting to work here, I wouldn't want to go hang out with the secretaries. I thought like . . . one woman pulls, like, two people pull out their needle-point. I'm just, like, appalled. And yet I think it's . . . I've gotten to know some of them better and I've sort of lost that attitude a little bit. I really like a lot of the women I work with and think they're really great human beings. They're doing these jobs that aren't that great, but a lot of them are single mothers and this is it. The only way they can bring the money home.

Kimberly reported a similar strategy:

> It could just be me. But I do feel myself getting defensive about this is just something I'm doing, you know, to earn some money and fill in time until I figure out how to get to point A or I can get another interview. I want people to know that I'm not interested in being a secretary. I'm not interested in just doing this. And there have been a couple . . . especially in some of the larger companies where I was filling in for the secretaries. Some of the other female secretaries even try to pull you into their circles. "Oh, you don't have any, not higher ambitions, but other aspirations, than we do." "Oh, you're going to be a secretary too! Wouldn't you like to stay here and work with us?" "No, I'm sorry. I wouldn't."

Like the cover story, these avoidance patterns say, "I am different. I am not a temporary or secretary in training. I keep my distance because I have nothing in common with you."[14]

The need for differentiation from and avoidance of permanent secretaries was particularly prominent among the college-educated female temporaries I interviewed. Aware of the large gap between their work expectations and work realities, and acutely conscious of the conflation of "traditional" femininity with the secretarial role, they found association with permanent secretaries threatening. Note, for example, how the stereotypical feminine activity of needlepoint is denigrated. Many of the women I interviewed did not want to end up in the pink-collar clerical army and consequently eschewed activities (at least in the workplace) that they found congruent or resonant with stereotypical images of femininity. The singly stigmatized female temporaries, then, may have been avoiding the double stigma of being both female and a secretary (see Kowalewski 1988).[15] The fear of fitting in or belonging was far greater than the fear of being seen as other and isolated.

In addition to avoidance, temporaries sometimes appraised the permanent staff in ways that emphasized their own differences and superiority. Bobby Jean, for example, viewed the educational or intelligence level of permanent employees as lower than her own: "And a lot of them could hardly read and write. I really didn't feel that a lot of them were very well educated. I got along with them, but they weren't people I wanted to hang around with or anything." Temporaries also criticized the way the permanent staff dressed and completed their work. Through devaluing the permanent employees, temporaries attempted to increase the evaluation of their own merits and enhance their sense of personal worth.

At Least I'm Not a Lifer

Besides directly avoiding interactions with the permanent office inhabitants, temporaries, instead of bonding together, also often avoided one another. Other temporaries, presumed to be real temporaries or "lifers" who were truly deviant and lacked the maturity, ambition, or ability to secure and hold down a real job, were to be shunned. "People who just do this all their lives! I just want to say, 'You poor things. Where are you going with your life?' You know? If you have a husband or a wife who's bringing in the basis of the cash and this is just something fun for you, then great, great. But if this is your entire life" (Steve). Whether or not it exists, the lifer does fulfill the role of an oppositional other. Through comparison to this oppositional other who embodies and merits all the derision, stigma, and low status accorded temporaries generally, individual temporary workers can deny their own deviance. Temporaries, through articulating the stereotype of the lifer to self and others, highlight their individual differences and thus their individual worth.

It's Only for the Day

Forgoing the possibility of building a supportive audience, temporaries who pursue a strategy of avoidance and self-isolation must instead simply "grin and bear it" (see Eggleston 1990; Kanner 1990).[16] Focusing on one's own cover story, the insignificance of the work to one's self-concept, and the finite nature of the assignment allows temporaries to "get through it." Kara, for example, articulated this approach:

> If I had my way in life, I would do commercials and film work and never have to do . . . lift my finger. So I take it with a grain of salt, because I know this isn't what I want to do. So when I'm folding envelopes and stuff and just feeling like a peon, you know, after a few days, going, "God, when am I going to get out of here?" I just realize that it's not my life's work and I really don't care. And I'm never going to have to see these people again.

Daniel recommended this strategy to me as a way of protecting the self:

> You cannot think of yourself as a lawyer or a doctoral candidate. You have to think of yourself as Kevin who is such-and-such and such-and-such. Because let's say you lose the job or you don't go through with . . . what are you? There's nothing. You have to rely on you, that inner you, that self, that's there. If you have a temporary job, you can't think of yourself as . . . you'll go batty. I'm a human being. This is what I'm doing this week. And you distance yourself as much as you can from the job, be-

cause you don't want to get involved. It's just stressful. And you don't want to play those games. You just want to go there, do your work, and get out.

"It's only for the day" or "it's only for another week" are the refrains temporaries repeat to themselves when the going gets rough. When the work is tedious and alienating, when the supervisor is condescending and rude, when the hours are long and the pay is low, temporaries can rest assured that things will change. Thus, by focusing on the "temporary" character of their work, their lack of personal commitment to it, and their alternative identity, temporaries can make it through assignments, collect their paychecks, and move on.[17]

It Could Be Different, Couldn't It?

There is nothing intrinsic about clerical work, however, that dictates that it look and feel demeaning and dehumanizing. This particular way of organizing and staffing the office is neither natural nor inevitable. It is a product of certain historical, political, and economic forces and relations. It is, in other words, a social construction, a construction that is recreated daily as people are ordered, scheduled, and report to work as temps.

Change from the Outside: Policies

One way in which temporary employment could be transformed is through policy initiatives. Policies that encourage and facilitate the creation of "good" full-time or permanent work opportunities, while discouraging economic incentives to cut costs through using "cheaper" temporary employees for positions that would otherwise be full-time, would be a step in the right direction (9 to 5 1986; U.S. House 1988). Involuntary temporary employment could be reduced or eliminated through the requirement that temporaries be given the same access to legal, political, and institutional protections as other workers. In essence, temporary work could be transformed by curtailing its disproportionate growth and eliminating its use as a routine staffing tool.

Temporary work could also be influenced through direct legislative efforts. In 1988 Representative Patricia Schroeder introduced the ill-fated Part-Time and Temporary Workers Protection Act, H.R. 2575, as part of the Economic Equity Act (U.S. House 1988). The bill called for prorated health and pension benefits for all employees working less than full-time if the employer provided these plans to their full-time employees (that is, part-time or temporary employees who worked half-time would receive half the employer-sponsored contribution to the benefit plans). Through extending health and pension benefits to contingent workers, the bill sought to provide protections for people who really wanted to work less than full-time as well as attempted to reduce the economic incentives for replacing full-time employees with peripheral workers. Similar bills directed at such parity between workers could be introduced at the local and state levels and reintroduced at the national level.

Beginning with government (city, state, and national) as an exemplar of rights and obligations centering on work, meaningful reforms could immediately be implemented. The federal Office of Personnel Management's implicit and explicit approval of "in-name-only" temporary positions as a cost-cutting measure, for example, could be changed through a repeal of the original ruling that allows the classification of federal employees as temporary for up to four years (9 to 5 1986; U.S. House 1988). Additionally, government could provide prorated benefits to those workers whose positions are truly temporary and short-term. Furthermore, the hiring practices of many businesses and corporations with government contracts for services from custodial to construction work could be influenced by requiring, as a condition of all agreements, that a reasonable ratio of peripheral to core workers not be exceeded (9 to 5 1986).

Another, more systemic approach to changing temporary work is to break or weaken the historical linkage between employment and "benefits" in the United States, particularly health care. Access to medical care in the United States has largely been defined as a privilege or benefit of employment rather than a right of citizenship, but this arrangement hasn't been working very well recently. In 1987 two-thirds of the estimated 34 to 40 million Americans with no health insurance coverage were workers (U.S. House 1988, 56). The number of workers without health insurance—predominantly those in the rapidly growing, low-paying, peripheral labor market—has been rising. Since 1981 there have been one million fewer workers covered under employer-provided health benefits each year (U.S. House 1988, 21). An economically viable and universal health care plan serving all citizens, regardless of employment status, would remove employers' economic incentive to create a two-tiered economy based on the cost of health care benefits.[18]

In addition, implementing economically viable flexible work schedules and providing affordable and appropriate systems of child and elder care would release many individuals, primarily women, from the unenviable position of "choosing" temporary or other forms of contingent employment out of necessity. The Conference Board, for example, observed: "Employers often think people 'really prefer' the only choice available to them. In this case, less employment regularity may be the only option open in today's labor market" (quoted in 9 to 5 1986, 10). Nearly 35 percent of women working part-time said that they would work more hours if affordable day care were available (9 to 5 1986, 10).

Change from the Inside: Collectivization

Change from the outside is not the only way in which temporary work could be transformed: it is also possible to imagine change coming from within. One way to pursue such change would be for existing unions or collective bargaining bodies to negotiate clauses requiring reasonable ratios of peripheral to core workers. Existing unions could demand that positions that are essentially full-time in content or duration be staffed accordingly (9 to5 1986; Christensen 1987). Additionally, rather than abandoning temporary workers to have them later become the Achilles' heel of labor (as full-time unionized workers are displaced by "cheaper," nonunionized temporaries, part-timers, and homeworkers), "authentic" temporary workers and their concerns could be treated as part of all ongoing labor negotiations (9 to 5 1986). Unions could also demand and back legislative efforts that require parity in pay, benefits, and working conditions for all contingent workers.

Temporary workers' dissatisfactions and complaints about low pay and poor working conditions could be the seeds of a collective response or rebellion among temporaries. Particularly within subpopulations of temporary workers (such as those in the theatrical and academic worlds), the sustained contacts between people who share the experience of temporary employment, necessary for organizing, are minimally available. Kara, for example, an actress who reported that she rarely met other temporaries on the job, said, "God. Everybody I know temps. Everybody." In the context of her non-wage-work activities in the theater world Kara met and interacted with numerous other temporaries. These alternative settings, then, could be the sites of an emerging common consciousness, collaboration, and the development of temporary unions and associations.

Obstacles to Change

Changes in government policies or regulations affecting the temporary industry face significant political barriers. U.S. businesses have been quite successful at resisting government regulations (environmental rules, worker safety regulations, and the like) through claiming they impose undue economic hardships and will ultimately result in the loss of jobs. The Dayton Tire Company, for example, when confronted with a directive demanding improvements in safety practices that the company maintained were cost-prohibitive and unnecessary, closed its doors, throwing its entire work force into unemployment (Verhovek 1994). In a period of high unemployment these scare tactics can be quite effective. Therefore, it is unlikely that the government would sponsor legislation requiring prorated benefits or other reform measures.

In addition, the current deficit and budgetary problems make it doubtful that government will lead the way in either eliminating its own exploitative use of workers in nominally temporary positions or providing prorated benefits. Any efforts to raise taxes or cut other programs to pay for this employment policy change would be resisted or would come at a high political cost. Yet these current government practices make leaders highly vulnerable to charges of hypocrisy.

Changes in temporary employment through collective action with full-time workers are similarly inhibited. The relatively small proportion of office workers now unionized and the decline of unions generally do not bode well for temporaries' automatic inclusion into existing collective bargaining agreements. In addition, full-time and temporary workers, protecting and augmenting their individual status through stigmatizing each other, often fail to recognize their common interests vis-à-vis management. As workers are divided and controlled on the basis of gender, race, and ethnicity, so too can they be divided on the basis of job categories and occupational status (Edwards and Gordon 1975; Piven and Cloward 1977).

Furthermore, temporary workers are extremely difficult to organize (9 to 5 1986). Not only are temporaries atomized and isolated through high turnover rates, constantly fluctuating schedules, and shifting work sites, but their identity management strategies are also ultimately individualistic, working against solidarity. The "temporary" of temporary work is a useful identity resource only when one truly believes that one's position is short-term; in order collectively to demand change, temporary workers would have to embrace the temporary role as their own. At present, temporary workers are far too isolated from one another and far too busy avoiding identification as "just a temp."

"How Would You Like to Work Here Full-Time?"

Even if temporaries fought for and won full parity in wages and benefits or were able to secure nominally temporary positions on a full-time basis, the current organization of clerical work is often a diminished and diminishing one. The respective fates of temporary and permanent workers in routine clerical work were revealed in an exchange I had with Ms. Brown, a full-time data entry clerk:

> Ms. Brown spoke to me occasionally after the first few days. One day she looked up and asked me, "How would you like to work here full-time?"
> I smiled and told her, "Uh, . . . no thanks."
> She laughed gently and said, "I hear you, I hear you."

Ms. Brown may have had benefits and more stability, but our gallows humor laid bare the ugly truth: no one, even those in them, liked these single-task, routine jobs very much.

Similarly, though temporaries rated coverage or secretarial placements more highly than routine assignments, these positions also had serious limitations. The work was not necessarily unskilled, but opportunities for increasing one's responsibilities over time were often severely restricted. Upward mobility for secretaries was often linked to the upward (or downward) mobility of their bosses rather than to rewards for their own work effort (see Kanter 1977). Consequently, many permanent workers in elite secretarial positions advanced rapidly, then all too soon found themselves pushing at the glass ceiling, a fate many temporaries recognized and wanted desperately to avoid.

Although a real workers' revolution, one that wrested control from management, could transform the very nature of office work, it doesn't seem to be on the horizon. Olivia, in lieu of a revolution and confronted with a lifetime of clerical work, attempted pragmatically to redefine, lower, and shift her expectations about the meaning of work in her life: "I don't really look to work as my sense of fulfillment. . . . I see the temp assignments, the secretarial type work, as a means to provide an income, but that's it. I mean, it doesn't really give me any satisfaction at all. . . . It's just a job."

Notes

1. The problems of accessing information through participant-observation methods on the job have also been noted by other researchers. Ely Chinoy (1955), for example, abandoned the participant-observation portion of his research on automobile workers after a brief period: "A job in the plant was part of the original research plan; since 1946 was a time of labor shortage and high turnover, there was no difficulty in securing employment in the factory. Only a few weeks were spent in the plant, however, because it soon became evident that the circumstances of work on the assembly line to which I was assigned made it difficult to talk to other men or to pay attention to much more than the work itself" (27).

2. The inherent transience, seasonal fluctuations, and ambiguous boundaries of the temporary work force made finding a stable population from which to interview random individuals difficult. Temporary agency rosters would have eliminated some of this difficulty, but I was unable to obtain access to such lists. Therefore, I used a modified snowball sampling strategy beginning with several unconnected individuals, often temporaries I met on assignment. I asked each interviewee for assistance in locating additional temporary workers to interview. In general, my respondents were from middle-class backgrounds and highly educated. More than two-thirds of my respondents had earned a bachelor's degree. Undoubtedly, my methods for contacting and recruiting respondents (a reliance on voluntarism rather than a subject stipend, for example) affected the types of temporary workers I was able to interview. Thus, although I had initially hoped to interview an educationally, racially, and age diverse group, my respondents were less diverse on the

whole than the temporary employment sector generally. The interviews, which typically lasted one to three hours, were principally conducted in person, although in three instances interviewees requested phone interviews because of geographical and time exigencies. I followed an open-ended interview schedule, addressing issues and themes that I had identified as salient from my participant-observation experiences and from preliminary interviews. I pursued new topics when they arose and shared my own experiences as a temporary when appropriate. Often my respondents were more interested in talking about their other pursuits, dreams, and aspirations during the interview. What I originally perceived as difficulty keeping the interview "on track," I eventually came to see as one of the more interesting aspects of the research. Just as I came to each interview with a particular set of motivations, my respondents also had an agenda. I believe I represented a sympathetic ear, someone who would take their complaints about temporary work seriously and reflect back to them an alternative, more desired, image of self. I enlisted "respondents." My respondents enlisted an "assistant" in the social construction of an alternative self. I tape recorded and transcribed all interviews, where permission to do so was granted (in all cases except one) and offered each interviewee a complete transcript and the opportunity to clarify or elaborate on our conversation. Besides giving me an incentive to transcribe the interviews quickly, the transcript review provided further contact with the interviewee during which I could ask follow-up questions or get referrals and additional assistance. The names of individual temporary workers, temporary counselors, client company supervisors, and some of the client companies are pseudonyms.

Chapter 1

1. The employee leasing industry has come under criticism and regulation as insurance fraud and mismanagement have left many workers without the health or other employee benefits they were promised (see Meier 1992).

2. Casual or day labor, of course, is not a new phenomenon. I am referring to the establishment and growth of an industry that matches employers and casual laborers for profit.

3. This is a small sampling of the personnel available as represented in the advertising copy from Crain's Directory of Temporary Services (1990, 62–63).

4. A relatively high degree of concentration exists among the industry leaders. These three firms, among others making up the top 1 percent of the industry—those establishments employing one thousand or more people each—controlled 34 percent of the temporary market. Indeed, four-fifths of the entire industry's receipts were billed by just eleven firms in the late 1970s (Harrison and Bluestone 1988, 212).

5. A little over a century later, in 1992, women constituted 81.3

percent of file clerks, 89.8 percent of data entry clerks, 83.5 percent of general office clerks, 95.1 percent of typists, 99 percent of secretaries, and 97.3 percent of receptionists (U.S. Department of Commerce 1993, 406).

6. The typewriter, successfully mass produced and introduced to the office in the 1880s, produced an entirely new category of clerical workers named for the machines they operated: typists (Davies 1974, 1982).

7. In many industries, such as banking and typesetting, technological innovation has been closely followed by feminization (Prather 1971; Davies 1982; Cockburn 1983, 1985; Fine 1990; Goldin 1990).

8. Braverman's insight, that the reorganization of clerical work under the efficiency experts often resulted in a reduction in the size of the clerical work force, probably still pertains: "The secretarial function is replaced by an integrated system which aims at centralized management, the breakdown of secretarial jobs into detail operations subdivided among production workers, and the reduction of the number of secretarial workers to one-half, one-quarter, or even smaller fractions of their former number" (Braverman 1974, 346–47). The new "efficient" hierarchical organization of labor (even if it did not include the entire clerical sector) reduced staffing overall.

9. Hewlett-Packard, among other companies, explicitly acknowledges the use of an in-house floater pool to buffer its full-time employees from market forces and improve morale (Waller 1989).

10. Corporate decisions to contract out all services deemed unnecessary to the "core" business—such as cafeteria, janitorial, and mail services—have led to larger numbers of part-time and other contingent workers. The contract companies providing these business services typically hire part-time and contingent workers (U.S. House 1988).

11. The Joint Partnership Training Act, under the assumption that temporary work is equivalent to job training, allows unemployment offices to refer people to temporary agencies that do not charge a fee. Client companies then qualify for government training subsidies for hiring referred temporary workers. Many state unemployment offices have adopted referrals to temporary agencies as standard practice (Gonos 1992).

12. Current Internal Revenue Service code (section 414) requires that temporary employees who work "substantially full-time" (defined as 1,500 hours or more during a twelve-month period) must be included in any pension plans for which they are otherwise qualified. Manpower argues that this section, which was designed to protect temporary employees, actually hurts them since in practice client companies terminate long-term assignments just short of the 1,500-hour maximum, creating periods of unemployment for individual workers (U.S. House 1988). From the perspective of the client company, however, a position that is essentially full-time can be staffed more cheaply by a series of low-cost temporary employees.

Chapter 2

1. A list of twenty-eight Right temporaries "given honorary mention for meritorious service" in *The Right Approach* in the fall of 1990, for example, lists only three men (Right Temporaries, Inc., 1990). (I have counted only the traditionally "masculine" names—John, George, and Paul. Two more gender-neutral names—Pat and Chris—appear on the list, but even if they are included, there is still a preponderance of female names.) Additionally, of the six temporary secretaries pictured in Manpower's benefits brochure, all are women in their thirties and all but one are white (see U.S. House 1988, 167–72). This pattern is consistent across other published lists of temporaries in other temporary agency newsletters.

2. College students are reminded of the "many" presumed nonmonetary or future monetary rewards of their temporary employment, primarily acquiring skills, connections, and experience for postgraduation "real" employment. The president of one agency, for example, advises the parents of college students to take an interest in their students' careers by supporting temporary work over other forms of summer employment: "Perhaps working downtown or in the suburbs as a receptionist, mailroom clerk, typist or telemarketer in a major Fortune 500 company might be considered more constructive than building hot dogs" (Right Temporaries, Inc., Spring/Summer 1991, 1). Perhaps. Yet all these work assignments pay little more than food service and are not necessarily routes to higher-paying, higher-status positions.

3. Howe (1986, 46) notes the "relatively high proportion of black temporary workers," however, without a similar choice-based explanation.

4. Similarly, Lillian Rubin noted in *Worlds of Pain* (1976) the routine responses she was offered as opposition to the women's movement by working-class women: "As if reciting a litany, several women spoke the same words over and over— 'I like a man to open the car door and light my cigarettes.' Upon closer questioning about the importance of these two behaviors, one woman laughed then admitted, 'I've gotta admit, I don't know why I said that. I don't even smoke' " (131–32).

5. The paradox here is that most temporary workers unquestioningly accept and exaggerate the prevalence of this stereotypical temporary worker yet assert that they, their friends, and acquaintances working as temporaries are not like lifers at all. Like the earnest narrator of ghost stories at summer camp, temporaries seem to say, "Just because you've never seen one doesn't mean they don't exist." To be fair, a small percentage of workers probably fit the lifer stereotype (Wendy, for example, as a "counselor," had worked with temporary workers with emotional disorders and substance abuse problems: "I had to go, literally go, to a client's premises to escort someone out, because they were sleeping in the conference room. I mean, this person had slurred words.") What is problematic and most compelling about the category of the lifer, however, is its persistence and the disproportionate emphasis and attention it receives.

6. The lifer, an exaggerated and problematic category, is the embodiment of the stereotypical bungling temporary worker (underqualified, unprofessional, and unemployable). Long-tenured temporaries, it is presumed, must have done something to deserve their occupational fate. In her study of laid-off and downwardly mobile managers, Katherine Newman (1988) describes this deeply entrenched cultural tendency to attribute either high or low position in the social structure as "meritocratic individualism": "At the center of this doctrine is the notion that individuals are responsible for their own destinies. This idea, which owes its origin to Calvinist theology, carries into the world of work a heavy moralism. One's occupation, or more precisely one's career or trajectory within an occupation, are viewed as a test of commitment, and the product of hard work and self-sacrifice. Cast this way, success is not a matter of luck, good contacts, credentials, or technical skill but is a measure of one's moral worth, one's willingness and ability to drive beyond the limitations of self-indulgence and sloth" (Newman 1988, 76). The laid off can redeem themselves, avoiding negative assessments of their worth by themselves or by others, if they "land on their feet" and quickly secure a comparable or better job. The longer one remains unemployed, the more the original layoff will be perceived as a judgment or revelation of serious characterological flaws.

7. In order to become a member of Equity, one must be involved in paid theatrical work for a particular period of time. This creates a "catch-22" situation for actors, since paying, non-Equity acting work is scarce.

8. This cliché was spoofed in Richard Greenberg's play *Eastern Standard* when a character summoned the waitress in a New York restaurant by calling out "actress" (Greenberg 1989).

9. The extent to which graduate students relied on temporary employment as a means of summer support became abundantly clear to me shortly after I began this research. When I discussed my research in classes, workshops, or informal graduate student gatherings, those in attendance would regale me with stories of their temporary experiences. And near the end of academic quarters or years I would receive telephone calls from a wide range of students soliciting recommendations for "good" temporary agencies.

10. Universities, often accused of being ivory towers removed from the concerns of the real world, have been subjected to many of the same economic forces driving corporate downsizing and shifts to contingent staffing. New tenure-track (core) academic positions are scarce (Magner 1994). Newly minted Ph.D.'s in English, for example, routinely compete with eight hundred to a thousand other applicants for each available tenure-track position (Nelson and Bérubé 1994, B[1]). Similarly, Robert Zimmer, the chair of the mathematics department at the University of Chicago, reported receiving between six hundred and seven hundred applications during recent tenure-track departmental searches (Magner 1994, A[17]). Adjunct and visiting (peripheral) positions, however, appear to be on the rise. Indeed,

nearly 40 percent of faculty positions in the United States today are part-time (Nelson and Bérubé 1994, B[3]). In such a crowded market, universities can find any number of qualified applicants willing to teach courses on a contingent basis.

Chapter 3

1. The average hourly earnings for all Chicago clerical temporaries in 1987 was $6.30. Data entry workers, general clerical workers, and messengers earned an average of $5.37 an hour; receptionists earned slightly more per hour at an average of $5.89; and secretaries, typists, and word processors earned an average of $7.61 an hour (U.S. Department of Labor, Bureau of Labor Statistics, 1988, 27).

2. By 1992, however, the temporary industry (at least in New York) was enjoying a postrecession resurgence of work orders. One temporary counselor noted, "I'm sending out temps now who hadn't worked for me in two or three years" (Berck 1992, 10[F]).

3. Greta Foff Paules (1991), in her study of waitresses in New Jersey, argues that the waitresses exercised considerable autonomy from management dictates primarily because of a severe labor shortage in the local area; the knowledge of bountiful employment opportunities elsewhere made exit a viable option.

4. Temporary employment was experienced as more flexible when blocks of time were taken off. Temporaries who wanted and could afford part-year schedules did take long periods of time off. Moreover, though temporaries may be constrained to the "normative" forty-hour work week, permanent workers are often required to work far longer than that (Schor 1991). In a labor market in which forty hours plus per week is standard, freedom from additional hours may be interpreted as flexibility. Employers may resist granting extensive leaves—paid or unpaid—for full-time workers. The political battle over family-leave legislation was one indicator of employers' resistance to even unpaid employee time off (Devroy 1990; Taylor 1991; Pine 1992). Although the trade-off may not seem economically rational, at least some temporaries may be buying more time off by forgoing employer-sponsored benefits, job security, and higher wages.

5. One temporary worker, informed of my study by her agency, told me that she had agreed to be interviewed solely to ensure a positive relationship with her counselor. At first I thought of this event only as a methodological and ethical problem, but later my interpretation evolved to view it as another example of the uncertainty, dependency, and vulnerability of temporary workers in their relationship to their agency.

6. Agencies request client companies to submit work reviews on their temporary employees. At the agency where I did the majority of my field work, for

example, each client was sent a "Quality Control Report" asking for rankings, from below average to superior, on qualities such as cooperation, appearance, speed, accuracy, reliability, and punctuality.

7. Temporary agencies could have simplified accounting procedures by providing paid lunch time (through lowering hourly rates), but there were several incentives for them to maintain the current time and pay system. One incentive was to create the appearance of higher hourly wages for prospective temporaries. Another incentive, however, was that by maintaining the majority of the temporary work staff as "part-time," agencies could avoid unemployment insurance claims. Existing unemployment legislation covers only full-time employees, defined as those who work forty-plus hours per week. By disenfranchising their temporary staff of unemployment insurance benefits, agencies could minimize their operating costs.

8. Trent, for example, described how he was found out after he had "gone permanent" with a client company he had entered as a temporary: "When I finally took a full-time job, it was with a company the temp agency had sent me to. And they knew about it. One day after I'd quit with them they called the company and asked for me. They didn't say who they were, and of course the switchboard transferred them to me. They were, like, 'You signed a contract that said you wouldn't take full-time work from one of our clients. I suggest you make sure that they pay the fee to us.' And I told them, 'Look, these people were nice enough to let me come in here and use their computer to work on my résumé, and I don't appreciate you hassling them.' That got them. They didn't believe me and accused me of lying, but I just said, 'Hey, prove it.' They even went so far as to bill the company for my services, but eventually they dropped it."

9. The president of Manpower has estimated that one-third of all Manpower temporary employees depart the agency payroll to accept permanent jobs annually—"very frequently with people to whom we've assigned them" (U.S. Department of Labor, 1988, Women's Bureau, 95).

10. The temporary agency actively discourages the hiring of "their people" by client companies (see Parker 1994). Client companies must agree to pay the temporary agency a finder's fee for any temporary worker they hire from the agency's payroll. In practice, however, this fee is often negotiable: "It depends on the client whether we charge a finder's fee. Sometimes the client is a real large user of our services, a big law firm that works with us, gives us a lot of orders. We won't charge them a finder's fee at all. But our standard policy is if the company decides to hire someone, it's 75 percent of that individual's first month salary on a permanent basis" (Cindy). Nevertheless, some temporary workers believed that they had lost permanent positions based on the disincentive of their agency's finder's fee. It is possible that the finder's fee prevents some client companies from approaching "good" temporary workers with full-time work offers.

Chapter 4

1. Client companies, like the government, were beginning to use a series of long-term temporaries rather than filling certain coverage positions with full-time workers. Aleshia, for example, had worked in the same communications company for more than six months at the time of our interview. Although the position required, and she was given, a great deal of responsibility, the company was neither searching for a full-time employee nor considering offering the position to Aleshia on a permanent basis. Indeed, she had been informed that company executives had instituted a hiring freeze.

2. Debbie's division hired workers from a number of different agencies that used their own pay rates. Thus, temporaries working together, doing the same work, discovered that they were receiving different hourly rates. Those who were receiving lower wages began agitating for comparable (higher) wages.

3. Such assignments also required physical stamina. The physical effects of repetitive clerical work are an important aspect of temporary work. Judy, for example, noted the physical costs of working at the video display terminal (VDT) for an entire day (a fate she, unlike many temporary workers, had been mostly able to avoid through switching off with another temporary): "With this data entry we're just entering information. There's one girl and I, we share the terminal. In the morning I may verify reports from the day before and then in the afternoon I switch and input data. I feel a little bit more comfortable because it is tedious just sitting at those things for eight hours a day. Yesterday I stayed on it all day, and at the end of the day my eyes were burning. But when you switch jobs, you don't get as tired during the day. And you don't say, 'Oh God, I got to go back to this tomorrow.'" Negative health effects, including repetitive motion trauma (Randolph 1989; Streitfeld 1991; Adler 1992; Galen 1992) and eye strain injuries (Roan 1993), have recently been noted among workers who spend a large proportion of their work day engaged in VDT work. Given their routine and repetitive work tasks, temporary workers may be at high risk for these injuries.

4. Word processing in some organizations was coming under new pressures of standardization and routinization. In one large Chicago law firm, for example, secretaries (temporary or otherwise) were instructed to use company-created templates when producing documents. Typing in "memo," "letter," "deposition," or other standard document names called up a preformatted shell document into which information was typed: "You just type 'letter' and it will come up on the screen as a template. And if you have any problems, they have a help desk. So if you don't know how to do anything, you call up and 'How do you set up columns?' They'll tell you. It's not hard. It's not hard at all" (Lillian). The computer network system allowed even minor document formatting decisions to be made centrally. Thus secretaries were divested of one more area of decision making and expertise.

5. The absence of sociability, a detriment to workers, may be seen as an advantage to management. Westwood, for example, noted how women workers in a British hosiery factory resisted management control through a shopfloor culture rich in friendships, pranks, gossip, and celebrations. These forms of resistance were primarily collective activities: "There were no 'laffs' to be had on your own: bunking off to the toilets, spending too much time in the coffee bar made no sense if it was an individual activity; there was no way to organise a prank without your mates or to have a laff at a pornie picture or a coarse joke. The material base for all of these was the friendship group" (Westwood 1984, 91). Because temporaries do not know others, they have fewer opportunities to "steal" an extra moment on break, lunch, or at the copy machine than more connected, socially embedded, permanent employees.

6. This form of organizational isolation in work is not unique to temporary work. Note, for example, the isolation of the full-time and permanent clothing grader and telephone operator: "One male grader described his former manual job in a men's wear factory, where he worked in a room with 1,000 other employees and was able to call across the tables, or walk here and there for a chat. . . . He contrasted this with his present work at Newstyle in a small secluded computer room, where the operators sit at their scopes, back to back, more cut off than before from each other and the rest of the world. 'Basically, it's a fairly boring job, it's very similar, you do the same thing every day. You don't get to meet anyone. It's just you and your computer and that's it' " (Cockburn 1985, 25). "I've worked here almost two years and how many girls' first names do I know? Just their last name is on their headset. You might see them every day and you won't know their names. At Ma Bell they speak of teamwork, but you don't even know the names of the people who are on your team" (Terkel 1972, 66). Many other workers in routinized jobs, particularly those who must be on headsets or always at a computer (switchboard operators, reservationists, telemarketers, and the like), are isolated from their co-workers during the course of their daily working lives.

7. Chinoy (1964) noted that permanent workers in the automobile factory that he studied resisted transfer between jobs. Management interpreted this resistance as workers' "satisfaction" with their present positions, but Chinoy argued that it was because there was little to be gained and much to be lost by moving: "In the automobile industry, shifting from one assembly-line job to another often offers little long-run improvement at the same time that it may, in fact, create difficulties for the worker. Since each job is likely to demand different kinds of movements, and therefore call upon different muscles, the first few days on a new assignment are often accompanied by a good deal of muscular soreness and stiffness. . . . Resistance to changing jobs, therefore, does not necessarily mean that workers are satisfied with what they are doing—or even 'adjusted' to it. It may reflect rather an understandable reluctance to undertake the often difficult task of learning a new job that frequently offers no real advantage over the old one" (1964, 70). Other analysts (Friedmann

1955, 1961; Westwood 1984) noted that workers' resistance to changing jobs was related to a reluctance to leave their work group or work mates behind.

8. Integration and embeddedness in sociability routines and social networks for temporaries, however, can also have costs: "Sometimes it's hard. When I left Rose University it was very difficult, because I had been there six months, long enough to get very well acquainted with them. And they were actually my friends by the time I left, and that was kind of rough. In fact, I have to go back there and see those guys" (Bobby Jean).

9. The unintended consequences of intensive control appear frequently in the workplace (Garson 1975; Glenn and Feldberg 1982; Ferguson 1984). Intensive formal control of the work process tends to become self-reinforcing. Removing workers' internal motivation through minimizing their autonomy, in other words, can also be counterproductive and inefficient for management. Besides the drains imposed on management or supervisory resources when temporaries withdraw from the work, discontented and alienated workers can become active office pirates or saboteurs (Ferguson 1984). Petty theft, intentional misfiling, computer sabotage, breaches of confidence, or other workplace mischief, pursued as retribution, can impose losses on client companies: "I take some office supplies. But definitely. I feel like shit, man! I'm not getting anything else out of this job. No benefits. No nothing. No paid lunch. Nasty attitude. I think I can take all the pastel Post-Its I want. You know?" (Helen). "There's a memo on the computer with no password or lock on it. It's like a list of people that they could fire to save money. And I just wonder if John knows that, casually in a memo, his name was just thrown on this list of people that they might be able to get rid of to save some money. And I am really dying before I leave to print that memo up and stick it on his desk" (Patsy). Contrary to the win-win rhetoric of the temporary industry, then, both management and workers may lose when work is contracted on a "just-in-time" basis.

Chapter 5

1. Robin Leidner (1993), in her work on the routinization of interactive service work, describes these efforts to standardize people as "routinization through transformation." She argues that the maintenance of employers' control over worker-customer interactions is "not merely a matter of prespecifying workers' attitudes and demeanors on the job, but also of transforming the workers into the sorts of people who will make the desired decisions" (1993, 38). The temporary industry, however, particularly in a buyer's market, has little incentive to invest resources in socializing or transforming their temporary work force. Temporaries who already possess "good" phone manners and "proper" office etiquette and who dress "professionally," like those who already know word processing software, are

likely to be given preference over those needing assistance in developing these presentation skills.

2. Erving Goffman emphasized that humans, as social beings, each with an image of how he or she would like to be seen and known, attempt to control and manipulate the impressions they make on others (Goffman 1959, 1961, 1963). He named the collection of social techniques and strategies that individuals use to control or guide others' impressions "impression management" (Goffman 1959). Arlie Hochschild coined the term "emotional management" to denote those techniques and tactics that individuals use to control or manage their feelings "to create a publicly observable facial and bodily display" (1983, 7). "When rules about how to feel and how to express feeling are set by management, . . . when deep and surface acting are forms of labor to be sold, and when private capacities for empathy and warmth are put to corporate uses," the performances are "emotional labor" (Hochschild 1983, 89).

3. This focus on appearance and behavior is not specific to temporary workers, however. Permanent secretaries also faced these judgments as part of their work lives (see Kanter 1977).

4. Transgressions such as wearing the same clothing too frequently are highlighted when temporaries remain in long-term assignments. A smaller work wardrobe is sufficient when viewed only briefly in multiple work settings.

5. Some agencies actively encouraged temporaries to purchase new clothing through work performance reward programs (based on accumulated on-assignment hours or high marks on quality assurance cards) that awarded gift certificates from "good" department stores as prizes.

Chapter 6

1. Paradoxically, temporary work pursued as financial support for an alternative identity, as with sidebet temporaries (actors, artists, students), compromises and threatens that alternative identity. Work as a defining characteristic is difficult to fend off.

2. For example, "just a housewife," "just a laborer," "just a waitress." The qualifier "just" has no resonance when placed before high-status occupational titles. "Just a lawyer" or "just a doctor" seems almost nonsensical.

3. By "self-concept" I refer to an individual's sense of identity that emerges from social interaction with others, following Robert A. Scott in *The Making of Blind Men* (1969): "A man's self-concept consists of attitudes, feelings, and beliefs he has about the kind of a person he is, his strengths and weaknesses, his potentials and limitations, his characteristic qualities, and so forth. These things are expressed both in his actions and in his responses to the questions, 'Who am I?' and

'What kind of a person am I?' A man's self-concept, or his personal identity if you prefer, is at the heart of his experience as a socialized human being. His subjective experience of the world is colored by it; his actions and reactions to others are filtered through it; and his behavior in most situations is guided by it" (Scott 1969, 14–15). This self is an elaboration of Charles Horton Cooley's "looking-glass self" (1902) and George Herbert Mead's "self" (1934).

4. Scott argues that men with vision deficiencies are made into or socialized into "blind men" through contact with normals and blindness organizations that impute the social identity of "blind man" onto them: "All blind men respond to this identity in some way, even if only to dispute it; for those who internalize it, this putative social identity becomes a personal identity" (1969, 20).

5. Lingo or argot has frequently been noted as an important support for particular identity constructions. For example, medical students revel in their new-found professional/scientific lingo: it constructs an "in" professional group as well as an "out" lay group. Temporaries, then, sharing in the lingo of the industry of their temporary assignment, could construct themselves to self and others as "understanders" and part of the "in" group.

6. Temporaries often bump up the skill level without a corresponding increase in compensation. Thus, the client company may get a word processor at the hourly rate of a receptionist or a computer consultant/trainer at the hourly rate of a word processor.

7. Linguists have particularly noted these verbal techniques in women's speech patterns (Henley 1977).

8. Fred Davis, in an examination of the strained interaction between the disabled and normals, argues that a "breakthrough" may occur when enough redefinitional work is completed that normals may relate to the disabled as individuals: "In moving beyond fictional acceptance what takes place essentially is a redefinitional process in which the handicapped person projects images, attitudes and concepts of self which encourage the normal to identify with him (i.e., 'take his role') in terms other than those associated with imputations of deviance" (1961, 127).

9. Goffman argues that people with an "immediately apparent" stigma may attempt to introduce other social information about themselves to counter or minimize their stigma: "It is a fact that persons who are ready to admit possession of a stigma (in many cases because it is known about or immediately apparent) may nonetheless make a great effort to keep the stigma from looming large. The individual's object is to reduce tension, that is, to make it easier for himself and the others to withdraw covert attention from the stigma, and to sustain spontaneous involvement in the official content of the interaction" (1963, 102). Temporaries, particularly on the job with people who "know" that they are temporary, may nevertheless attempt to downplay the significance of their temporary status.

10. Chinoy argued that autoworkers tried "to maintain the illusion

of persisting ambition by defining their jobs in the factory as 'temporary' and by incessantly talking of their out-of-the-shop goals and expectations" (1955, 123): "By emphasizing to their fellows the strengths of their intentions and the ripeness of their plans, workers seek to elicit one another's respect. Since high value is placed upon achievement of out-of-the-shop goals, those who seem on the verge of leaving in order to start a business may gain increased prestige. Men spoke frequently and enviously of their co-workers who seemed near achievement of some out-of-the-shop goal. Yet concomitantly the spuriousness and unreality of much of this talk was frequently recognized. . . . Talk of leaving may therefore be double-edged: on the one hand it may elicit respect, on the other it may stamp one as an idle and unrealistic fellow who talks too much" (Chinoy 1955, 95). Based on the number of past workers who had fulfilled such dreams, however, Chinoy assumed that these goals were "at best temporary, at worst only a public demonstration that one is ambitious—which may convince others without assuaging inner feelings of guilt and self-blame" (1955, 123).

11. The use of props to support one's identity and fend off the depersonalizing aspects of psychiatric hospitals was recorded among pseudopatients in a study conducted by D. L. Rosenhan (1973). The pseudopatients, voluntarily committed, were to convince hospital staff of their sanity in order to leave. One pseudopatient, a student of psychology, requested that his textbooks be brought to the hospital even though this would have blown his cover as a researcher.

12. During interviews I was frequently enlisted as a supportive audience for people's cover stories. While I wanted to talk to people about their experiences of temping, they wanted to talk about their acting or musical careers, their goals and aspirations.

13. Andrea Fontana documented similar patterns of avoidance and differentiation among the unwilling patients of Sunny Hill convalescent home. He noted: "The interaction among patients is mainly characterized by its absence. Patients do not have anything to do with each other. To fraternize with other patients would mean to place oneself at their level, to admit that one indeed belongs here" (1977, 112).

14. I also found myself, even with the built-in incentives of my "research role," sometimes disassociating from others on the job. For example, this excerpt is from my field notes at a point where I felt I was learning little new information but desperately needed the additional income: "Now I seem to be withdrawing from the situation even when I'm at work or interacting; becoming very quiet, doing 'my job,' and getting the hell out of there as soon as possible. This is not necessarily beneficial for my 'research role.'"

15. Similarly, Mark R. Kowalewski argues that singly stigmatized gay men attempted to differentiate themselves from doubly stigmatized gay men with AIDS: "AIDS threatens gay men with both physical danger and double stigma. In

response, nearly all persons sought to put some kind of barrier between themselves and PWAs [persons with AIDS]; gays not only confronted the possibility that they might get sick and die, but that they might be forced to assume the social stigma of AIDS. The thought that 'I' might get AIDS, that AIDS 'looks like me,' was a reality perhaps too painful and too costly for gays to readily accept" (1988, 223).

16. Avoidance strategies lend credence to the stereotype of the sullen temporary secretary with an attitude problem. Matt Groening (1986), for example, lists the "sullen temporary" as one of the "81 Types of Employees" in a cartoon from *Work Is Hell*. Similarly, attempts to prop up alternative identities may lead temporaries to engage in "forbidden" behaviors (such as personal phone calls, writing projects, or escapist reading on company time), which are then interpreted as confirmation of existing negative stereotypes about the workers and their work ethic.

17. During their tenure temporaries used different identity management strategies at different times. It is possible that finely tuned adjustments (according to each specific work environment) were made, but based largely on my own experience of the work, I believe that these strategies were undertaken sequentially. Green temporaries would attempt to pass or blur the lines of their temporary role. A more seasoned temporary, becoming more defensive, would begin to tell the cover story. And veteran temporaries, at their most discouraged, would disassociate themselves from their work and from stigmatized others.

When I first began working as a temporary, I decided, for methodological reasons, that I would play it straight and not reveal that I was researching temporary work while on assignment. Instead, I would do the best job that I could and observe as much as possible without assistance from either my agency representatives or client company supervisors. As the work became more tedious and I began to experience firsthand the erosion of my self-esteem, I abandoned this resolve and began telling my graduate-student cover story to anyone who would listen. (I did not mention that I was conducting field work on temporary work, however, unless asked directly about my research.) Near the end of my tenure as a temporary, when I felt I was learning very little new but still needed the income, I found myself behaving sullenly and avoiding contact with others on the job.

18. National health care reform seriously appeared on the government's legislative agenda in 1994 for the first time since the early 1970s. Yet President Clinton's proposed health care plan, as well as several other Democratic proposals, maintained the strong historical connection between employment and the provision of health care. Most of these proposals advocated employer mandates that would have required businesses to pay a percentage of the health insurance premiums for their employees, but the legal definition of an "employee" would not have covered all workers. For example, businesses would have been exempt from paying premiums for independent contractors—potentially providing further economic incentive for coercing workers into becoming nominally self-employed (Pear 1994; see also Linder 1992).

References

Adler, Jerry. 1992. Typing without keys: An epidemic of injuries among office workers prompts a search for a better keyboard. *Newsweek,* 7 December, 63–65.

Anderson, Gregory. 1976. *Victorian clerks.* New York: Kelley.

Ansberry, Clare. 1993. Workers are forced to take more jobs with few benefits: Firms use contract labor and temps to cut costs and increase flexibility. *Wall Street Journal,* 11 March, 1(A), 4(A).

Asinof, Lynn. 1988. Rent-an-exec firm. *Wall Street Journal,* 4 August, 1(A).

Barrett, Michelle, and Mary McIntosh. 1980. The "family wage": Some problems for socialists and feminists. *Capital & Class* 11 (Summer): 51–72.

Barrier, Michael. 1989. Temporary assignment: Guy Milner foresees a dynamic economy propelled by workers who haven't put down roots. *Nation's Business* 77 (October): 34–37.

Bassett, Joan. 1989. Fidelity Investments brings temporary employment in-house. *Personnel Journal* 68 (December): 65–69.

Becker, Howard S. 1963. *Outsiders: Studies in the sociology of deviance.* New York: Free Press.

Belous, Richard S. 1989a. *The contingent economy: The growth of the temporary, part-time, and subcontracted workforce.* Washington, D.C.: National Planning Association.

———. 1989b. How human resource systems adjust to the shift toward contingent workers. *Monthly Labor Review* 112 (March): 7–12.

Benet, Mary Kathleen. 1972. *Secretary: Enquiry into the female ghetto.* London: Sidgwick & Jackson.

Bensman, David, and Roberta Lynch. 1987. *Rusted dreams: Hard times in a steel community.* Berkeley: University of California Press.

Berck, Judith. 1992. Filling the gaps in the post-recession work force. *New York Times,* 26 April, 10(F).

Berger, Suzanne, and Michael Piore. 1980. *Dualism and discontinuity in industrial society.* Cambridge: Cambridge University Press.

Bernstein, Harry. 1992. Workers at Caterpillar lost a battle, but the war goes on. *Los Angeles Times,* 28 April, 3(D).

Blin, Dick. 1987. Steelworkers give up jobs, work rules, money, benefits, holidays to USX. *Labor Notes* 96 (February): 1.

Bluestone, Barry, and Bennett Harrison. 1982. *The deindustrialization of America: Plant closings, community abandonment, and the dismantling of basic industry.* New York: Basic Books.

Bowles, Samuel, David Gordon, and Thomas Weisskopf. 1983. *Beyond the waste land: A democratic alternative to economic decline.* New York: Anchor.

Braverman, Harry. 1974. *Labor and monopoly capital.* New York: Monthly Review Press.

Brock, William E. 1987. They're not 'McJobs.' *Washington Post,* 11 June, 23(A).

Carey, Max L., and Kim L. Hazelbaker. 1986. Employment growth in the temporary help industry. *Monthly Labor Review* 109 (April): 37–44.

Cavett, Dick. 1990. My union, Actors' Inequity. *New York Times,* 10 August, 17(A).

Chafe, William H. 1972. *The American woman: Her changing social, economic, and political roles, 1920–1970.* New York: Oxford University Press.

Chinoy, Ely. 1955. *Automobile workers and the American dream.* Boston: Beacon Press.

———. 1964. Manning the machines: The assembly line worker. In *The human shape of work: Studies in the sociology of occupations,* ed. Peter L. Berger, 51–81. South Bend, Ind.: Gateway.

Christensen, Kathleen. 1987. Women and contingent work. *Social Policy* (Spring): 15–18.

———. 1991. The two-tiered workforce in U.S. corporations. In *Turbulence in the American workplace,* ed. Peter Doeringer, 140–55. New York: Oxford University Press.

Cockburn, Cynthia. 1983. *Brothers: Male dominance and technological change.* London: Pluto Press.

———. 1985. *Machinery of dominance.* Boston: Northeastern University Press.

Cohen, Laurie P. 1988. Use of legal temps is on the rise—but practice faces bar challenges. *Wall Street Journal,* 12 May, 25(W), 25(E).

Cohen, Stephen S., and John Zysman. 1987. The myth of a post-industrial economy. *New York Times,* 17 May, 2(F).

Cohn, Samuel. 1985. *The process of occupational sex-typing: The feminization of clerical labor in Great Britain.* Philadelphia: Temple University Press.

Cook, Christopher. 1994. Temps: The forgotten workers. *The Nation,* 31 January, 124–28.

Cooley, Charles H. 1902. *Human nature and social order.* New York: Scribner.

Costello, Cynthia B. 1989. The clerical homework program at the Wisconsin Physicians Services Insurance Corporation. In *Homework: Historical and contemporary perspectives on paid labor at home,* ed. Eileen Boris and Cynthia R. Daniels, 198–214. Urbana: University of Illinois Press.

Crain's Directory of Temporary Services. 1990. *Crain's Chicago Business,* 28 May, 62–63. Chicago.

Creative downsizing. 1992. *Personnel Journal* 71 (September): S08.

Crompton, Rosemary, and Stuart Reid. 1982. The deskilling of clerical work. In *The degradation of work? Skill, deskilling, and the labour process,* ed. Stephen Wood, 163–78. London: Hutchinson.

Crozier, Michel. 1971. *The world of the office worker.* Chicago: University of Chicago Press.

Davies, Margery. 1974. Woman's place is at the typewriter: The feminization of the clerical labor force. *Radical America* 8 (July–August): 1–37.

———. 1982. *Woman's place is at the typewriter: Office work and office workers, 1870–1930.* Philadelphia: Temple University Press.

Davis, Fred. 1961. Deviance disavowal: The management of strained interaction by the visibly handicapped. *Social Problems* 9 (May): 120–32.

Day, Jeff S. 1988. Employee leasing. In *Flexible workstyles: A look at contingent labor,* 59–64. U.S. Department of Labor, Women's Bureau. Washington, D.C.: GPO.

Devroy, Ann. 1990. President vetoes bill on unpaid family leave. *Washington Post,* 30 June, 4(A).

Doeringer, Peter. 1991. *Turbulence in the American workplace.* New York: Oxford University Press.

Doeringer, Peter, and Michael Piore. 1971. *Internal labor markets and manpower analysis.* Armonk, N.Y.: M. E. Sharpe.

Economic Development Commission of the City of Chicago. 1990. *Chicago Economic Update.* 2 (Spring). Chicago.

Edwards, Richard, and David Gordon. 1975. *Labor market segmentation.* Lexington, Mass.: Lexington Books.

Eggleston, Kirk. 1990. Working one day at a time: The best thing about a job as a "temp" is that it doesn't last. *Washington Post,* 2 September, 5(B).

Feinstein, Selwyn. 1989. More small firms get help from rent-a-boss service. *Wall Street Journal,* 5 January, 1(B).

Feldberg, Roslyn L., and Evelyn Nakano Glenn. 1983. Technology and work degradation: Effects of office automation on women clerical workers. In *Machina ex dea: Feminist perspectives on technology,* ed. Joan Rothschild, 59–77. New York: Pergamon Press.

Feldman, Stuart. 1990. Companies buy into employee leasing plans. *Personnel* 67 (October): 1–2.

Ferguson, Kathy E. 1984. *The feminist case against bureaucracy.* Philadelphia: Temple University Press.

Fine, Lisa M. 1990. *The souls of skyscrapers: Female clerical workers in Chicago, 1870–1930.* Philadelphia: Temple University Press.

Fischer, Claude S. 1982. *To dwell among friends: Personal networks in town and city.* Chicago: University of Chicago Press.

Fontana, Andrea. 1977. *The last frontier.* Beverly Hills, Calif.: Sage.

Freedman, Audrey. 1985. *The new look in wage policy and employee relations.* New York, N.Y.: Conference Board.

Freudenheim, Milt. 1992. Health costs up 12.1 percent last year, a study says. *New York Times,* 28 January, 2(C).

Friedmann, Georges. 1955. *Industrial society: The emergence of the human problems of automation.* New York: Free Press.

———. 1961. *The anatomy of work: Labor, leisure, and the implications of automation.* New York: Free Press.

Galen, Michele. 1992. Repetitive stress: The pain has just begun; as workers' injuries mount, VDT makers face an onslaught of suits. *Business Week,* 13 July, 142–53.

Gannon, Martin J. 1974. A profile of the temp help industry and its workers. *Monthly Labor Review* 97 (May): 44–49.

———. 1978. An analysis of the temporary help industry. In *Labor Market Intermediaries,* special report no. 22, 195–255. Washington, D.C.: National Commission for Manpower Policy.

———. 1984. Preferences of temporary workers: Time, variety, and flexibility. *Monthly Labor Review* 107 (August): 26–28.

Gannon, Martin J., and Uri Brainin. 1971. Employee tenure in the temporary help industry. *Industrial Relations* 10 (May–June): 168–75.

Garson, Barbara. 1975. *All the livelong day: The meaning and demeaning of routine work.* New York: Penguin Books.

———. 1988. *The electronic sweatshop.* New York: Penguin Books.

———. 1992. Permanent temps. *The Nation,* 1 June, 736–37.

Glenn, Evelyn Nakano, and Roslyn L. Feldberg. 1979. Proletarianizing clerical work: Technology and organizational control in the office. In *Case studies on the labor process,* ed. Andrew Zimbalist, 51–72. New York: Monthly Review Press.

———. 1982. Degraded and deskilled: The proletarianization of clerical work. In

Women and work, ed. Rachel Kahn-Hut, Arlene Kaplan Daniels, and Richard Cloward, 202–17. New York: Oxford University Press.

Goffman, Erving. 1959. *The presentation of self in everyday life.* New York: Anchor Books.

———. 1961. *Asylums: Essays on the social situation of mental patients and other inmates.* New York: Anchor Books.

———. 1963. *Stigma: Notes on the management of spoiled identity.* Englewood Cliffs, N.J.: Prentice-Hall.

Golden, Lonnie, and Eileen Appelbaum. 1992. What was driving the 1982–88 boom in temporary employment? Preferences of workers or decisions and power of employers? *American Journal of Economics and Sociology* 51 (October): 473–93.

Goldin, Claudia. 1990. *Understanding the gender gap: An economic history of American women.* New York: Oxford University Press.

Gonos, George. 1992. Temporary trouble. *The Progressive* 56 (October): 15.

Gose, Ben. 1994. More jobs? Liberal-arts graduates still find prospects dim. *Chronicle of Higher Education* 18 May, 28–30(A).

Gottfried, Heidi. 1992. In the margins: Flexibility as a mode of regulation in the temporary help service industry. *Work, Employment & Society* 6 (September): 443–60.

Greenberg, Richard. 1989. *Eastern standard.* New York: Dramatists Play Service.

Greenhouse, Steven. 1992. The union movement loses another big one. *New York Times,* 19 April, 1(E).

Groening, Matt. 1986. Chapter 4: The 81 types of employees. In *Work is hell.* New York: Pantheon Books.

Grossman, Morton E., and Margaret Magnus. 1989. Temporary services: A permanent way of life. *Personnel Journal* 68 (January): 38–40.

Halcrow, Allan. 1988. Temporary services warm to the business climate. *Personnel Journal* 67 (October): 84–89.

Harrison, Bennett, and Barry Bluestone. 1988. *The great U-turn: Corporate restructuring and the polarizing of America.* New York: Basic Books.

Hartmann, Susan M. 1982. *American women in the 1940s: The home front and beyond.* Boston: Twayne.

Helliker, Kevin. 1991. Personnel trap: Some injured workers learn the hard way they aren't insured. *Wall Street Journal* 19 March, 1(A).

Henley, Nancy M. 1977. *Body politics: Power, sex, and nonverbal communication.* Englewood Cliffs, N.J.: Prentice-Hall.

Hinds, Michael deCourcy. 1992. Graduates facing worst prospects in last two years. *New York Times,* 1 May, 1(A).

Hochschild, Arlie Russell. 1983. *The managed heart: Commercialization of human feeling.* Berkeley: University of California Press.

Howe, Wayne J. 1986. Temporary help workers: Who they are, what jobs they hold. *Monthly Labor Review* 109 (November): 45–47.

Hughes Everett C. 1945. Dilemmas and contradictions of status. *American Journal of Sociology* 50 (March): 353–59.

———. 1984. *The sociological eye.* New Brunswick, N.J.: Transaction Books.

Hulin, Charles L., and Paul A. Joray. 1978. A survey of the socio-economic aspects of temporary work in the United States. In *Temporary work in modern society, Part II: Temporary work within a socio-economic framework,* ed. W. Albeda and G. M. J. Veldkamp. Deventer, Netherlands: Kluwer.

Impoco, Jim. 1993. Experimenting with test-tube temps: Even scientists can't find permanent jobs today. *U.S. News & World Report* 115 (October 11): 70.

Joray, Paul A. 1972. The temporary industrial labor service market in the Chicago and St. Louis metropolitan areas. Ph.D. diss., University of Illinois at Urbana-Champaign.

Kanner, Bernice. 1990. Peon for a day. *New York,* 2 April, 41–44.

Kanter, Rosabeth Moss. 1977. *Men and women of the corporation.* New York: Basic Books.

Katz, Harry. 1985. *Shifting gears: Changing labor relations in the U.S. automobile industry.* Cambridge: MIT Press.

Kessler-Harris, Alice. 1982. *Out to work: History of wage-earning women in the United States.* New York: Oxford University Press.

Kilborn, Peter T. 1993. New jobs lack the old security in time of "disposable workers": The forty-hour week, with benefits, is in decline. *New York Times,* 15 March, 1(A), 6(A).

———. 1994. College seniors finding more jobs but modest pay: A permanent change? *New York Times,* 1 May, 1(A), 17(A).

Kirkpatrick, David. 1988. Smart new ways to use temps. *Fortune,* 15 February, 110–14.

Kornbluh, Joyce L. 1988. Historical perspectives on part-time and temporary workers. In *Flexible workstyles: a look at contingent labor,* 14–20. U.S. Department of Labor, Women's Bureau. Washington, D.C.: GPO.

Kowalewski, Mark R. 1988. Double stigma and boundary maintenance: How gay men deal with AIDS. *Journal of Contemporary Ethnography* 17 (July): 211–28.

Kutscher, Ronald E., and Valerie A. Personik. 1986. Deindustrialization and the shift to services. *Monthly Labor Review* 109 (June): 3–13.

Landers, Ann. 1989. Not wanted: Women jobhunters of fifty. *Chicago Tribune,* 5 June, 5(E).

Leidner, Robin. 1993. *Fast food, fast talk: Service work and the routinization of everyday life.* Berkeley: University of California Press.

Leone, Richard D., and Donald R. Burke. 1976. *Women returning to work and their interaction with a temporary help service.* Philadelphia: Center for Labor and Manpower Studies, Temple University.

Levin, Ira. 1972. *The Stepford wives.* New York: Random House.

Lewin, Tamar. 1994. Low pay and closed doors greet young in job market. *New York Times,* 10 March, 1(A), 12(A).

Linder, Marc. 1992. *Farewell to the self-employed: Deconstructing a socioeconomic and legal solipsism.* New York: Greenwood Press.

Lockwood, David. 1958. *Black-coated workers.* London: Allen & Unwin.

Luxton, Meg. 1980. *More than a labour of love: Three generations of women's work in the home.* Toronto: Women's Press.

Machung, Anne. 1983. Word processing: Forward for business, backward for women. In *Machina ex dea: Feminist perspectives on technology,* ed. Joan Rothschild, 124–39. New York: Pergamon Press.

Magner, Denise K. 1994. Job-market blues: Instead of the anticipated demand, new Ph.D.'s are finding few openings. *Chronicle of Higher Education* 27 April, 17–20(A).

Mamet, David. 1988. *Speed-the-plow.* New York: Grove Press.

Mangum, Garth, Donald Mayall, and Kristin Nelson. 1985. The temporary help industry: A response to the dual internal labor market. *Industrial and Labor Relations Review* 38 (July): 599–611.

McNally, Fiona. 1979. *Women for hire: A study of the female office worker.* New York: St. Martin's Press.

Mead, George H. 1934. *Mind, self, and society.* Chicago: University of Chicago Press.

Meier, Barry. 1992. Some "worker leasing" programs defraud insurers and employers. *New York Times,* 20 March, 1(A).

Mills, C. Wright. 1956. *White collar.* New York: Galaxy Books, Oxford University Press.

Moore, Mack A. 1963. The role of temporary-help services in the clerical labor market. Ph.D. diss., University of Wisconsin.

Morrow, Lance. 1993. The temping of America. *Time,* 29 March, 40–41.

Morse, Dean. 1969. *The peripheral worker.* New York: Columbia University Press.

Nardi, Peter, ed. 1992. *Men's friendships.* Newbury Park, Calif.: Sage.

National Geographic Society. 1990. *Imagine the mountain. . . .* Brochure. Washington, D.C.: National Geographic Society.

Negrey, Cynthia. 1990. Contingent work and the rhetoric of autonomy. *Humanity & Society* 14 (Winter): 16–33.

———. 1993. *Gender, time, and reduced work.* Albany: State University of New York Press.

Nelson, Cary, and Michael Bérubé. 1994. Graduate education is losing its moral base. *Chronicle of Higher Education,* 23 March, 1–3(B).

Newman, Katherine S. 1988. *Falling from grace: The experience of downward mobility in the American middle class.* New York: Vintage Books.

——. 1993. *Declining fortunes: The withering of the American dream.* New York: Basic Books.

9 to 5, National Association of Working Women. 1986. *Working at the margins: Part-time and temporary workers in the United States.* Cleveland: 9 to 5, National Association of Working Women.

——. 1987. *The service economy: Portrait of a new workforce.* Washington, D.C.: 9 to 5, National Associaton of Working Women.

Norwood, Janet L. 1987. The job machine has not broken down. *New York Times,* 22 February, 3(F).

Olesen, Virginia L., and Frances Katsuranis. 1978. Urban nomads: Women in temporary clerical services. In *Women working: Theories and facts in perspective,* ed. Ann H. Stromberg and Shirley Harkess, 316–38. Palo Alto, Calif.: Mayfield.

Pae, Peter. 1991. First Chicago cuts 1,000 jobs. *Wall Street Journal,* 25 July, 2(A).

Parker, Robert E. 1994. *Flesh peddlers and warm bodies: The temporary help industry and its workers.* New Brunswick, N.J.: Rutgers University Press.

Paules, Greta Foff. 1991. *Dishing it out: Power and resistance among waitresses in a New Jersey restaurant.* Philadelphia: Temple University Press.

Pear, Robert. 1994. Clinton health care plan poses question, "Who is an employee?" *New York Times,* 4 April, 1(A), 7(A).

Pine, Art. 1992. Congress approves family leave bill: Would allow workers up to twelve weeks of unpaid leave for family emergencies. *Los Angeles Times,* 11 September, 1(A).

Piore, Michael J., and Charles F. Sabel. 1984. *The second industrial divide: Possibilities for prosperity.* New York: Basic Books.

Piven, Frances F., and Richard A. Cloward. 1977. *Poor people's movements: Why they succeed, how they fail.* New York: Vintage Books.

Prather, Jane. 1971. When the girls move in: A sociological analysis of the feminiza-tion of the bank teller's job. *Journal of Marriage and Family* 33 (December): 777–82.

Pringle, Rosemary. 1988. *Secretaries talk: Sexuality, power, and work.* New York: Verso.

Randolph, Eleanor. 1989. Newsroom stress syndrome: Repetitive motions result in strains and injuries. *Washington Post,* 16 May, 9 (WH).

Reibstein, Larry. 1988. And now, "temp" managers: Firms use them to cut costs and make quick fixes. *Newsweek* (26 September): 52–53.

Right Temporaries, Inc. 1989a, 1990, 1991. *The Right Approach: The Publication for Professional Temporaries.* Chicago.

——. 1989b. *Welcome to Right Temporaries, Inc.* Organizational brochure. Chicago.

———. 1989c. *What does Right Temporaries, Inc. expect of me?* Organizational brochure. Chicago.

Roan, Shari. 1993. When it's all a blur. *Los Angeles Times,* 19 January, 1(F).

Rogers, Jackie Krasas. 1995. Just a temp: Experience and structure of alienation in temporary clerical work. *Work and Occupations* 22 (May): 137–66.

Rosenhan, D. L. 1973. On being sane in insane places. *Science* 179 (January): 250–58.

Rubin, Lillian B. 1976. *Worlds of pain: Life in the working-class family.* New York: Basic Books.

———. 1986. *Just friends: The role of friendship in our lives.* New York: Harper & Row.

Schor, Juliet B. 1991. *The overworked American: The unexpected decline of leisure.* New York: Basic Books.

Schwartz, Barry. 1973. Waiting, exchange, and power: The distribution of time in social systems. *American Journal of Sociology* 79 (January): 841–70.

Schwartz, John, Dody Tsiantar, Annetta Miller, Rich Thomas, John McCormick, Carolyn Friday, and Frank Washington. 1990. Young, gifted, and jobless. *Newsweek,* 5 November, 48–50.

Scott, Robert A. 1969. *The making of blind men: A study of adult socialization.* New York: Russell Sage Foundation.

Shelp, Ronald K. 1987. Giving the service economy a bum rap. *New York Times,* 17 May, 2(F).

Simonetti, Jack L., Nick Nykodym, and Louella M. Sell. 1988. Temporary employees: A permanent boon? *Personnel* 65 (August): 50–57.

Slaughter, Jane. 1986. ARMCO pact sets precedent: Plant by plant contracts. *Labor Notes* 82 (December): 16.

Sperry, Paul. 1993. Where are the full-time jobs? Firms hire more part-timers as regulations grow. *Investor's Business Daily,* 10 March, 1–2.

Spradley, James P., and Brenda J. Mann. 1975. *The cocktail waitress.* New York: John Wiley & Sons.

Streitfeld, David. 1991. Debating the perils of VDT's. *Washington Post,* 18 March, 5(D).

Strom, Sharon Hartman. 1992. *Beyond the typewriter: Gender, class, and the origins of modern American office work, 1900–1930.* Urbana: University of Illinois Press.

Taylor, Paul. 1991. Family-leave report creates commotion. *Washington Post,* 15 April, 7(A).

Ten Kate, Nancy. 1989. Here today, gone tomorrow. *American Demographics* 11 (December): 34–36.

Terkel, Studs. 1972. *Working.* New York: Avon Books.

Tilly, Chris. 1989. Half a job: How U.S. firms use part-time employment. Ph.D. diss., Massachusetts Institute of Technology.

Uchitelle, Louis. 1992. Pay of college graduates is outpaced by inflation. *New York Times,* 14 May, 1(A).

———. 1994. Job losses don't let up even as hard times ease. *New York Times,* 22 March, 1(A), 4(C).

U.S. Department of Commerce. Bureau of the Census. 1989a. *Here's the best temporary job in America.* Brochure. Washington, D.C.: GPO.

———. 1989b, 1990, 1991, 1992, 1993. *Statistical abstract of the United States.* Washington, D.C.: GPO.

U.S. Department of Labor. 1991. *Current business reports survey, 1990.* Bulletin 2413. Washington, D.C.: GPO.

———. Bureau of Labor Statistics. 1988. *Industry wage survey: Temporary help supply.* Bulletin 2313. Washington, D.C.: GPO.

———. Bureau of Labor Statistics. 1992. *Employment and earnings.* August.

———. Women's Bureau. 1975. *Handbook on women workers.* Bulletin 297. Washington, D.C.: GPO.

———. Women's Bureau. 1988. *Flexible workstyles: A look at contingent labor.* Washington, D.C.: GPO.

U.S. House. 1988. Employment and Housing Subcommittee. *Rising use of part-time and temporary workers: Who benefits and who loses?* 100th Cong., 2d sess., 19 May.

Verhovek, Sam Howe. 1994. Tire factory shuts doors in dispute over safety. *New York Times,* 20 April, 8(A).

Walker, Charles R., and Robert H. Guest. 1952. *The man on the assembly line.* Cambridge: Harvard University Press.

Waller, Larry. 1989. Here come the temps. *Electronics* 62 (May): 91–93.

Weitzman, Lenore. 1985. *The divorce revolution: The unexpected social and economic consequences for women and children in America.* New York: Free Press.

Werneke, Diane. 1984. *Microelectronics and office jobs: One impact of the chip on women's employment.* London: International Labour Office.

Westwood, Sallie. 1984. *All day, every day: Factory and family in the making of women's lives.* Urbana: University of Illinois Press.

Wiatrowski, William J. 1990. Family-related benefits in the workplace. *Monthly Labor Review* 113 (March): 28–33.

Wilkerson, Isabel. 1992. Refugees from recession fill hotel's payroll. *New York Times,* 1 March, 1(A).

Witchel, Alex. 1991. Ron Silver takes charge at Actors' Equity. *New York Times,* 14 October, 1(B).

Index